PERIOD FURNITURE
— PROJECTS —

PERIOD FURNITURE
— PROJECTS —

*Plans and full
instructions for
20 distinctive pieces*

— V. J. Taylor —

David & Charles

Dedication

This book is dedicated to my friend Dr James Campbell of Orlando, Florida, who is one of the finest non-professional cabinet makers I know; and to his wife Cornelia who dispenses real Southern hospitality!

Acknowledgements

Thanks are due to Sotheby's Press Office at Billingshurst and their Cheltenham office; also to Mallett & Son (Antiques) Ltd, and Mr John Biggs of J. Collins & Son, Bideford, for their help in supplying photographs. I am grateful, too, to Mrs Nicole Beckett for her assistance in producing the illustration for the front cover.

Photographs are reproduced by permission of the copyright holders: pages 7, 11, 22, 40, 47, 53, 60, 61, 73, 79, 93, 100, 113, Sotheby's, Billingshurst and Cheltenham; pages 16, 21, 101, 120, 126, Phillips Fine Art Auctioneers, London; pages 28, 80, J. Collins & Son, Bideford; pages 34, 86, Mallett & Son (Antiques) Ltd; pages 68, 106, the American Museum in Britain, Bath.

A DAVID & CHARLES BOOK
Copyright © V. J. Taylor, 1994
First published 1994

V. J. Taylor has asserted his right to be identified as author of this work in accordance with the Copyright, Designs and Patents Act 1988.

A catalogue record for this book is available from the British Library.

ISBN 0 7153 0085 7

Typeset by Ace Filmsetting Ltd, Frome Somerset
and printed in Germany by Mohndruck GmbH
for David & Charles
Brunel House Newton Abbot Devon

CONTENTS

INTRODUCTION

Over the past fifty years I have been privileged to supply designs to many fellow woodworkers by means of books or magazine articles, the great majority of which have been for period vernacular designs rather than the elaborate and ornate pieces that were custom-built for the aristocracy. The designs included in this book are all classics in their way which appealed to the general public of the time because of their attractive appearance combined with their utility. Many are still just as popular today.

Each project opens with a short historical note setting it in the background of its period, and some have been slightly modified in style, size, or decoration in order that they can be made up using modern methods or materials, or both. In many cases the method of construction is self-evident but in others it would be impossible to be certain without dismembering the piece – not a very practical proposition! Accordingly, in such cases, I have described the customary techniques found in pieces of similar style and from the same period.

I have assumed that the reader is already well versed in the basic skills of cabinet making and polishing. The Appendices have been included to cover the more unusual methods, and to avoid the constant repetition of elementary procedures. I hope that you will also find the illustrations and cutting lists useful. *Note that the first dimension in a cutting list always denotes the way of the grain.* Generous working allowances have been made to lengths and widths; thicknesses are net.

I have in all cases endeavoured to specify timbers and other materials which are widely available; it is very frustrating to get halfway through a project and find that a particular veneer, or an essential fitting, is no longer on the market. A list of suppliers is provided on pages 158–159.

Each project has been given a 'skill rating' of between 1 and 5, and the projects in each room section are listed in increasing order of difficulty. I hope this book will be a source of interest and enjoyment not only to the amateur woodworker but also to the professional producer of high-quality reproduction antique furniture.

CANTERBURY MUSIC RACK STAND

Although originally intended to hold sheet music, this early 19th-century design is equally at home today doing duty as a magazine and newsrack, and is well within the scope of most woodworkers.

A ccording to Thomas Sheraton, the name of this type of stand derived from the fact that the Archbishop of Canterbury ordered it first. Be that as it may, the design, and variations of it, are very popular today as newspaper and magazine racks. Our example is made entirely in mahogany and dates from about 1810. **Skill rating – 1.**

Corner posts (*part C*)

These are made from 1¼in (32mm) squares and the turning should be done first as the centres can be found easily before the posts are worked to a concave shape at a later stage. Fig 2(A) gives the pattern for the turning drawn on a grid of ½in (13mm) squares.

The next step is to shape the concave hollow at the upper end of each post, and Fig 2(B) and the corner plan in Fig 1 show the details. Most of the waste in the hollow can be sawn away as shown in the corner plan and the remainder cleared and shaped with a suitably sized gouge.

Divisions

The four curved rails (F) are straightforward as they are part of a regular curve which is 2½in (64mm) deep at its lowest point and

Fig 1 Perspective drawing of the carcase and framing plus corner-post detail. Some division rails have been omitted for clarity.

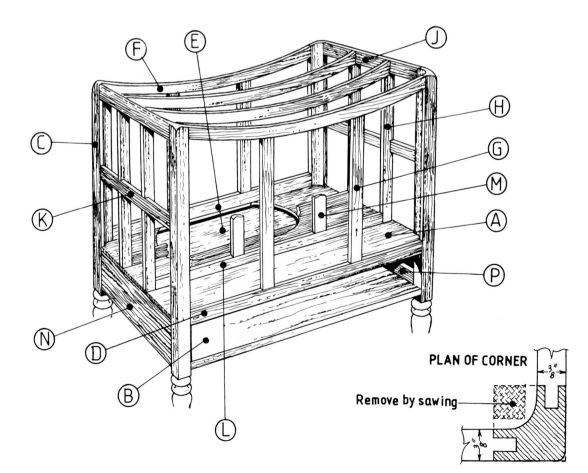

PLAN OF CORNER

Remove by sawing

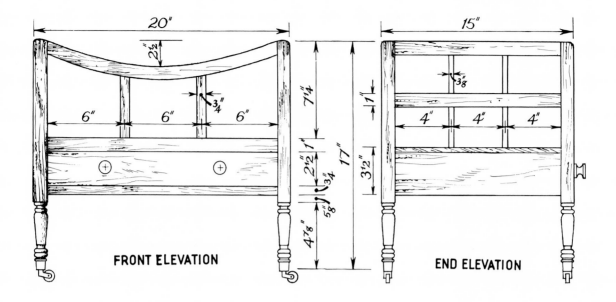

FRONT ELEVATION

END ELEVATION

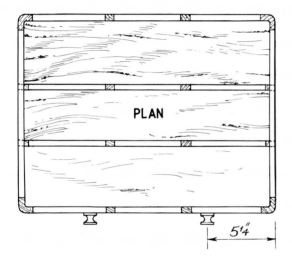

PLAN

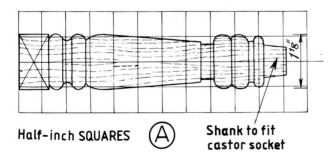

Half-inch SQUARES (A)

Shank to fit castor socket

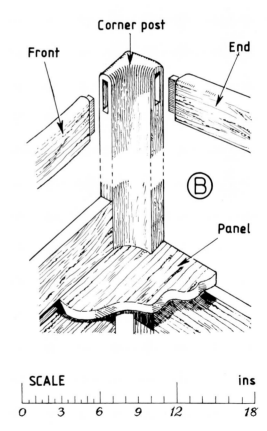

Corner post

Front

End

(B)

Panel

SCALE ins

0   3   6   9   12   18

Fig 2 Elevations and plan. (A) half-inch squared drawing of the turned section of a corner post; (B) detail of shaping on corner post.

they can be nested together when being marked out to save timber; they are mortise and tenoned into the corner posts (C). The vertical strips (G) at the front are mortise and tenoned into the frieze rail (D) at their lower ends and into the curved rails (F) at the top; their partners at the back are similarly jointed into the back panel (E).

There are two frame rails (L) which are glued and screwed to the panel (A) from underneath – which means that this job has to be done before fixing the panel to the ends (N). The rest of the joints are mortise and tenoned except for those where the vertical end strips (H) and the middle end rails (K) intersect, the former being notched around the latter.

The upper panel (A) laps over the end panels (N) and can be screwed and/or glue blocked to them, and is scribed at each corner to fit the concave shapes on the corner posts. The lower panel (B) can be lap-dovetailed to the drawer guides (P), which are screwed and glued to the corner posts and the inside of the end panels (N).

Drawer

This is conventional in style, the only noteworthy feature being that the dovetails have very narrow pins (called 'needle' pins) which are described in Appendix 1.

Brasswork

This comprises two plain brass circular knobs and four brass socket castors, all as shown in Fig 2.

Finish

Many readers will see the potential of the design as a modern news-cum-magazine rack and will be happy with one of today's plastic lacquer finishes; the appropriate antique finish would be a shellac-style one as described in Appendix 5.

Cutting List

	inches			mm		
	L	W	T	L	W	T
1 upper panel (A)	21	15½	⅜	534	394	10
1 lower panel (B)	21	16	⅜	534	407	10
4 corner posts (C), each	18	1½	1⅛	457	38	29
1 frieze rail (D)	21	1½	¾	534	38	19
1 back panel (E)	21	4	¾	534	102	19
4 curved division rails (F), each	21	3½	⅜	534	89	10
6 vertical frame strips (G) & (M), each	5	1	⅜	128	25	10
4 vertical end strips (H), each	7½	1	⅜	191	25	10
2 top end rails (J), each	15	1	⅜	381	25	10
2 middle end rails (K), each	15	1	⅜	381	25	10
2 central frame rails (L), each	21	1	⅜	534	25	10
2 end panels (N), each	15	4	¾	381	102	19
2 drawer guides (P), each	14	1	⅜	356	25	10
1 drawer front	18½	3	¾	470	76	19
2 drawer sides, each	14	3	½	356	76	13
1 drawer back	18½	3	½	470	76	13
1 drawer bottom	19	14	¼	483	356	6

Generous working allowances have been made to lengths and widths; thicknesses are net.

GEORGE III ELBOW CHAIR

A graceful chair, with touches of the Sheraton style about it, which dates back to the end of the 18th century. Probably made by a very competent country firm with the aim of producing a simplified version of a fashionable London design.

A pleasant design of about 1780 to 1790, made in mahogany, it is a much simplified version in the style of Sheraton with spade-toe legs and an upholstered sprung seat which has a slight serpentine shape at the front. The tops of the five narrow splads carry a stylized leaf design, and the crest or top rail is not only curved from top to bottom but also dished from end to end.

As a matter of historical interest, all chairs had arms until the end of the 16th century, when 'back stools' were introduced which, as their name implies, were stools to which backs had been added. In due course they underwent small alterations so that from the 18th century onwards they were known under several names such as single, side or parlour chairs.

Armchairs in which the arms extend fully to the front are, as Sheraton calls them, drawing room chairs. Elbow chairs such as this design where the arms are fixed to an arm stump set a few inches back from the front are, strictly speaking, writing or dining chairs because they can be pulled close to a table. **Skill rating – 3.**

Seat frame

Making spade-toe legs is described in the design for a serpentine-fronted sideboard (pages 54–55). At (A) in Fig 1 you can see how mortises need to be cut at the top squares of the legs to accept the mitred tenons on the side and front seat rails.

The most important joints are those where the side seat rails meet the backfeet, see Fig 1(B); for those who like historical accuracy, the mitred-tenon joints as employed at the front corners are the best ones to use. The method shown where the dowels on the back seat rail penetrate the tenons on the side seat rails is, in

Fig 1(A) joint construction at front corner; (B) suggested joint at back corner; (C) tenon shaped on top end of backfoot.

Arm stump

Front leg

Side seat rail

Notch

Seat bracket

(A)

Front seat rail

Backfoot

(B)

Back seat rail

Square tenon

(C)

Backfoot

my opinion, stronger and is known as a 'pinned' joint, but as dowels were not generally used until the 19th century (machine-made dowels were available from about 1850) the method is not strictly of the period.

The arm stumps are housed into the side seat rails as shown at Fig 1 (A), and screwed and glued in place: the screws can be driven either from the inside so that their heads will not be seen, or from the outside when the heads will need to be pelleted (see Appendix 1).

A large proportion of 17th and 18th century chairs did not have underframes and consequently the seat brackets shown in the front elevation and plan of the seat in Fig 2 and in Fig 1 (A) are essential to reinforce the seat frame. As you can see, they are glued and screwed into notches on the undersides of the rails; they must, of course, be kept low down in the frame so they do not make their presence felt through the upholstery.

Backfeet

The shape of these is shown on the squared-off drawing in the side elevation, Fig 2 – note that the grid comprises 2in (51mm) squares. To save timber they can be nested one into the other when marking them out (the arms and side seat rails can also be nested in a similar fashion).

In an effort to make the upper half of the backfeet appear lighter and more graceful the inner edges are bevelled off, starting from a point just above the stay rail: see the front elevation in Fig 2, and (B) on the 1in (25mm) squared-off drawing. Again to help the appearance, the backs are rounded off as in the side elevation; the feature is also shown at Fig 1 (B).

Four joints need to be made on each backfoot: one with the back seat rail (this has been dealt with already); another mortise to accept the tenon on the stay rail; a square tenon on the upper end which enters a mortise on the crest rail as illustrated at Fig 1 (C); and finally a small housing joint to fix on the arm, which is described in the next section.

Arm and arm stump

The shape of this can be plotted from the 2in (51mm) squared-off drawing in Fig 2, side elevation.

At the front end of each arm a hole needs to be bored to accept a pin which is turned on the end of the arm stump. At the junction with the backfoot the arm is notched in slightly and either a loose tenon or dowels may be inserted to strengthen the joint.

The pattern for the arm stumps is shown in the 1in (25mm) squared-off drawing in Fig 2 and the turning and reeding must, of course, be completed before fixing them. It is, however, advisable to fix the arms at both ends before shaping them with a spokeshave so they fair in neatly with both the stumps and where they join the backfeet.

Crest rails and splads

As already mentioned, the crest (top) rail is curved in two planes,

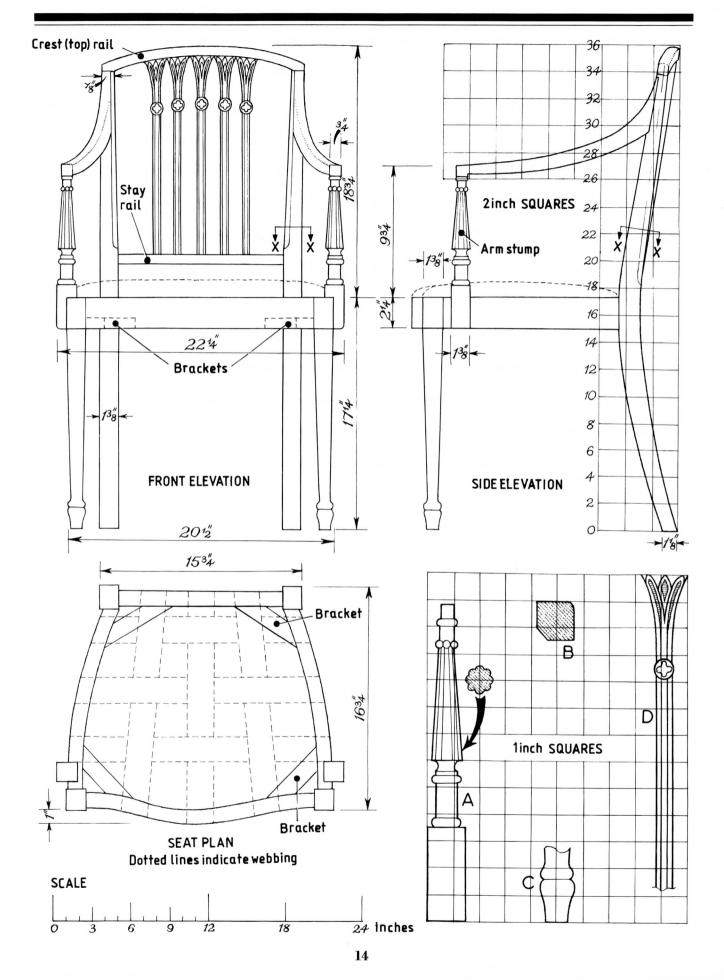

Crest (top) rail

Stay rail

$\frac{7}{8}$"

$\frac{3}{4}$"

$18\frac{3}{4}$"

$9\frac{3}{4}$"

$2\frac{1}{4}$"

$17\frac{1}{4}$"

$1\frac{3}{8}$"

$22\frac{1}{4}$"

Brackets

FRONT ELEVATION

$20\frac{1}{2}$"

2inch SQUARES

Arm stump

$1\frac{3}{8}$"

$1\frac{3}{8}$"

$1\frac{1}{8}$"

36 34 32 30 28 26 24 22 20 18 16 14 12 10 8 6 4 2 0

SIDE ELEVATION

$15\frac{3}{4}$"

$16\frac{3}{4}$"

1"

Bracket

Bracket

SEAT PLAN
Dotted lines indicate webbing

1inch SQUARES

A

B

C

D

SCALE

0   3   6   9   12   18   24 inches

Fig 2 Elevations and seat plan, plus squared-off details of shaped parts.

namely from top to bottom and front to back, the depth of the curve being 1in (25mm) in each case. A square mortise has to be cut at each end to accept the tenons on the ends of the backfeet, and also five small mortises for the tenons on the splads. As with the arms, it is best to fix the rail in position first before rounding it off with a spokeshave.

The five splads are similar but not identical as their lengths vary to follow the curve of the crest rail as does the carved decoration. This is illustrated at (D) in the 1in (25mm) squared-off drawing in Fig 2, and it should not be difficult to carve them with a combination of small chisels and gouges.

Upholstery

Fig 2 (seat plan) shows the disposition of the 2in (51mm) seat webbing, and full details of how to upholster this kind of seat are given in Appendix 6.

Finish

Although the heading illustration shows the chair finished in conventional shellac varnish, it would be acceptable and in period to paint it in a slightly off-white or light ivory colour, or even in black and embellish it with thin gold lines. Many chairs which were painted were made in beech throughout, and this timber is both cheaper and more easily obtainable than mahogany. In fact, even if the rest of the chair is of mahogany it would be worthwhile to use beech for the seat rails as it will accept tacks without splintering better than other woods.

Cutting List

	inches			mm		
	L	W	T	L	W	T
2 backfeet from one piece	38	6	1⅜	965	152	35
2 front legs, each	18	1¾	1⅜	457	45	35
1 front seat rail	21	2¾	1⅞	533	70	48
2 side seat rails from one piece	15½	2¾	3½	394	70	89
1 back seat rail	16	2¾	⅞	407	70	23
2 arm stumps, each	13	1¾	1⅜	330	45	35
2 arms from one piece	18	6½	⅞	457	165	23
1 stay rail	16	1⅛	¾	407	29	19
1 crest (top) rail	16	2	2	407	51	51
5 splads, each	16	2¼	⅝	407	58	16
4 seat brackets, each	7	1½	½	178	38	13

Generous working allowances have been made to lengths and widths; thicknesses are net.

POUCH WORK TABLE

*A pretty little work table that dates
back to the late 18th or early 19th
century — a time when all
genteel ladies were expected to be accomplished
needlewomen — and it would be
equally acceptable today.*

This attractive and useful little table dates back to the late 18th century and is made in satinwood. The screen can be raised at the back to shield the lady's face from the heat of the fire, and the pouch acts as storage space for the work in hand – embroidery, needlework, knitting, etc. The drawer can be withdrawn completely and put to one side and the side can be pulled out for needles, scissors, etc to be placed on it. **Skill rating – 3.**

General notes

The original design has been slightly modified to make construction more straightforward, and in particular the way in which the screen slides up and down has been altered so that the back legs taper for their whole length from the level of the carcase down to their toes, thus matching the front legs, which is not the case with the original piece. Note that all the legs are tapered on the inside faces only, a feature adopted by Thomas Sheraton in several of his designs for ladies' dressing and toilet tables.

Satinwood is in short supply these days except as veneer, but there are plenty of alternatives such as abura, afrormosia, cherry, guarea, sapele, or walnut; and if you are not concerned with authenticity you could use medium density fibre board (MDF) veneered with satinwood, lipping the edges where necessary.

Carcase

Since the top, back, ends and slide are comparatively small there is no reason why they should not be solid timber which will avoid a certain amount of framing up. The ends and back are mortised and tenoned into the legs (see Appendix 1 for details of the joint), as are the rails (F), (H), (I) and (J) (Fig 2); the end rails (G) are tenoned into the legs at the front but run over the tops of the back legs to which they are dowelled, so avoiding having to screw the hinges into end grain.

The screen slides up and down between the back (E) and the guide blocks (P); the latter are screwed and glued one at each end to the back legs as shown in the plan, Fig 1, and again in Fig 2.

Legs and underframe

As already mentioned, only the inner faces of the legs are tapered and they are otherwise completely plain, their toes being fitted into brass socket castors.

The underframe rails overlap in the form of a St Andrew's cross (sometimes called a 'saltire') and a halved joint is used where they intersect, as in Fig 3 (A). Fig 3 (B) shows the joint employed where the underframe meets the legs; a small pin can be driven in slantwise from underneath for extra strength.

Drawer

This is made in conventional fashion and is capable of being withdrawn completely. Its interior can be fitted as required to

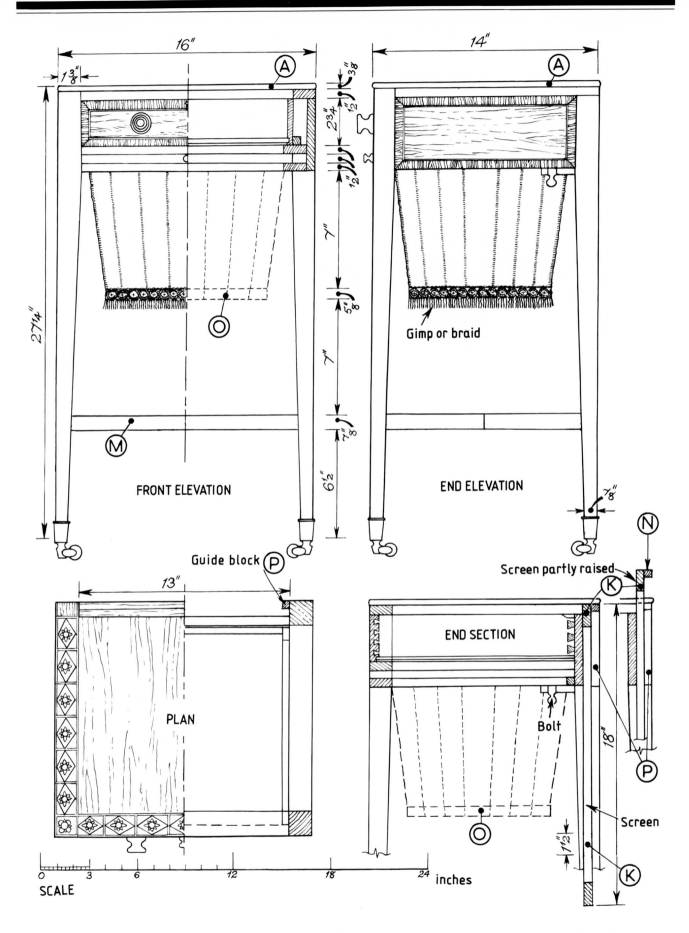

16"

1 3/8"

A

23 3/4"

3/8"

1/2"

1/2"

7"

5/8"

7"

7/8"

6 1/2"

27 1/4"

FRONT ELEVATION

M

O

14"

A

Gimp or braid

END ELEVATION

7/8"

N

Screen partly raised

K

Guide block   P

13"

PLAN

END SECTION

Bolt

18"

P

1 1/2"

Screen

K

O

0   3   6   12   18   24   inches

SCALE

Fig 1 Elevations, plan and end
section.

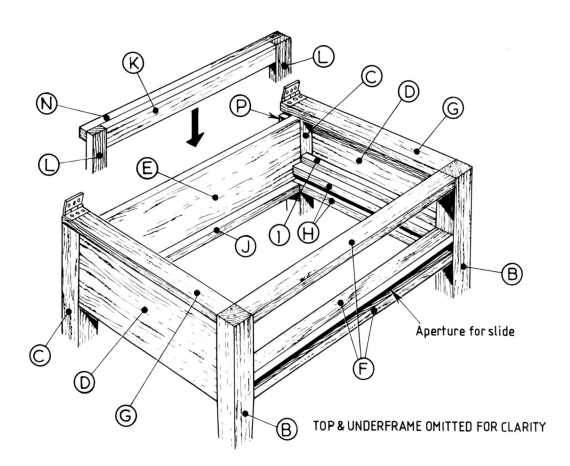

Aperture for slide

TOP & UNDERFRAME OMITTED FOR CLARITY

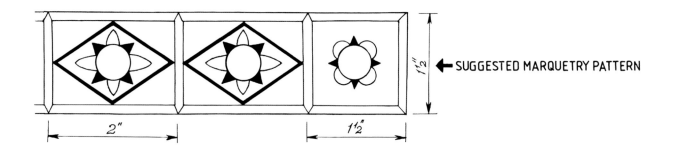

SUGGESTED MARQUETRY PATTERN

2"

1½"

1½"

Fig 2 Constructional drawing
and suggested pattern for
marquetry strip.

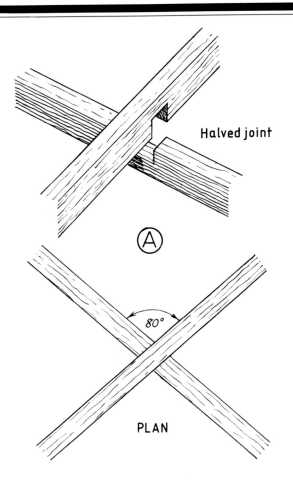

Halved joint

(A)

PLAN

80°

include provision for scissors, needles, pins, threads, wool, etc.

The slide is simply a piece of solid wood with a couple of small blocks pinned and glued to its back edge to prevent its being withdrawn completely.

Screen

Shown in detail in the end section of Fig 1 and in Fig 2, this is a simple rectangular frame mortised and tenoned together, and the fabric (which matches that of the pouch) is attached to the back with gimp pins; the pleating is optional. A strip (N) is pinned and glued to the back of the top edge and acts not only as a finger pull but also to prevent the screen from sliding down too far, coming to rest on the top end of a guide block (P) at each side. Two small brass bolts engage with holes at the bottom of the screen to hold it when it is in the raised position.

Pouch

This was usually made in silk; a manmade fabric could be today's alternative. The pleats are optional but desirable because the perimeter at the top is greater than that at the bottom, and the surplus fabric can be taken up in the pleats; the length required is best taken from the actual table when it has been assembled. The lower edge is tacked around the bottom block (O), which should preferably be beech as it holds tacks well: the upper edges are tacked to the inside of the rails (F), (H) and the tacking rail (J). Gimp or fringed braid can be fixed around the bottom with gimp pins to provide a finishing touch.

Decoration

Although the drawer front and the end panels shown in the elevations in Fig 1 are veneered and crossbanded, this can be dispensed with if you are using nicely figured solid wood.

The decorative strips at each side of the top can be assembled as marquetry before being glued down and a suggested pattern is shown in Fig 2; some veneers which would contrast well with that used in the main construction include ebony, holly, rosewood and satinwood. The two knobs on the drawer front and the single one for the slide are all turned from wood and embellished with a series of concentric circles on their faces.

Hardware

This comprises a box lock for the drawer and socket castors for the legs, all of which are easily obtainable.

Finish

The shellac varnish described in Appendix 5 would be suitable.

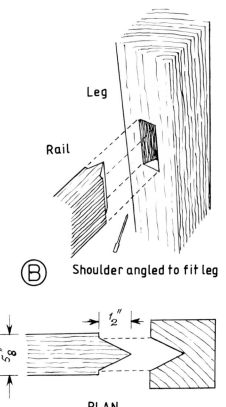

Leg

Rail

(B) Shoulder angled to fit leg

½"

⅝"

PLAN

Fig 3(A) halved joint used at the intersection of the underframe rails; (B) form of housing joint where the underframe rails enter the legs.

Cutting List

	inches			mm		
	L	W	T	L	W	T
1 top (A)	17	15	⅜	431	381	10
2 front legs (B), each	28	1¾	1⅜	711	45	35
2 back legs (C), each	27½	1¾	1⅜	698	45	35
2 end panels (D), each	13¼	4¾	⅝	336	121	16
1 back panel (E)	15½	4¾	⅝	394	121	16
3 front rails (F), each	15½	2	⅝	394	51	16
2 top end rails (G), each	14	2	⅝	356	51	16
4 inner end rails (H), each	13½	2	⅝	343	51	16
2 drawer guides (I), each	12½	1	⅝	318	25	16
1 tacking rail (J)	13½	1	⅝	343	25	16
2 screen rails (K), each	14	2	½	356	51	13
2 screen posts (L), each	16	2	½	407	51	13
2 underframe rails (M), each	19½	1⅛	⅝	492	29	16
1 screen strip (N)	14	¾	½	356	19	13
1 base for pouch (O)	11	10	⅝	279	254	16
2 guide blocks (P), each	5	¾	½	127	19	13
1 drawer front	14	3¼	⅝	356	83	16
2 drawer sides, each	13	3¼	⅜	330	83	10
1 drawer back	14	3¼	⅜	356	83	10
1 drawer bottom	13	13	¼	330	330	6

Generous working allowances have been made to lengths and widths; thicknesses are net.

SOFA TABLE

*A handsome table from the early
19th century which would lend grace
and interest to any room and at the
same time fulfil its original purpose as
an occasional table used in conjunction
with a modern settee.*

This type of table was a development of the well-known Pembroke table (see pages 47–52) and, as its name implies, was intended to be used in conjunction with a sofa; it was particularly useful for invalids, and Sheraton mentions in his *Cabinet Dictionary* that ladies used them to read, write, or draw upon. Sofa tables usually had two shallow drawers on one of the long sides, the opposite long side being made to show two dummy drawer fronts. The table illustrated is in mahogany with ebony stringing in the top and also in the corner blocks, while there are matching ebony beadings around the drawers. Its Regency style dates it to about 1810. **Skill rating – 3.**

Top

This consists of the centre bed plus the two leaves which are joined by rule joints; the leaves are supported by hinged brackets connected to the frame with knuckle joints, and details for making these are given in the design of the Pembroke table.

The grain of the bed and the leaves runs crosswise so that the rule joints can be worked along the grain and not across it, which could lead to problems; the outer edges are moulded to the double-reed profile shown in the inset drawing in Fig 1. You will probably find it best to work the edge mouldings first and then the rule joints; by doing this, any small chipping or splintering on the corners will be removed when the rule joint is cut.

A straight cutter which has a single flute with bottom cut used in a power router is the ideal tool for cutting the channels to accept the ebony stringing, and such cutters are available in $\frac{1}{16}$in (1.6mm), $\frac{5}{64}$in (2mm), and $\frac{1}{8}$in (3mm) diameters. Alternatively the channels could be worked by hand with a scratch-stock (see Appendix 3).

You may have to soak the stringing in hot water to make it flexible enough to go round the bends at the corners: make sure that the channel is of a size to allow the stringing to fit snugly but not tightly, otherwise the adhesive will be squeezed out.

Columns

These finish $2\frac{3}{4}$in (70mm) square, being turned from 3in (76mm) squares, and the pattern for the turned section is shown in the grid-drawing in Fig 1; a square tenon is left at the top and this is later wedged into the transverse rail (D) shown in Fig 3(A). Note that the wedges are aligned to be parallel to the grain of the rail so that if there is any shrinking, the effect will be to tighten the joint.

The 5in (127mm) at the lower end of each column has tapered dovetail slots cut into flat faces made on opposite sides as shown at Fig 3(E), and these accept matching dovetails worked on the ends of the legs. Ordinary parallel dovetails could be used, but by tapering them you ensure that the weight of the table itself tends to make the joint firmer – highly desirable in any design with splayed legs. In fact, the jointing of the legs should be further

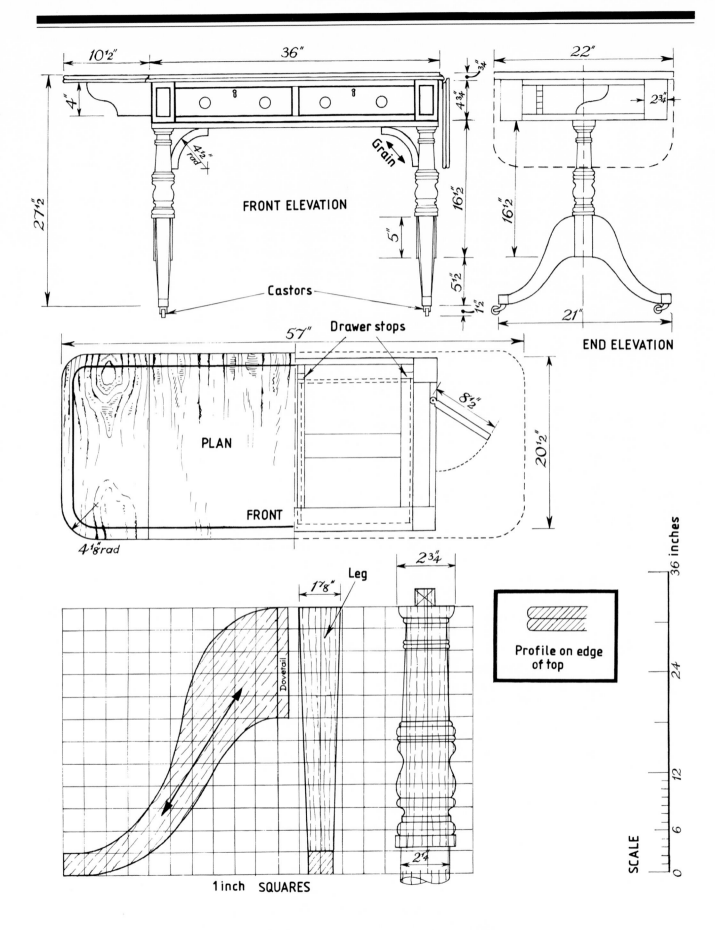

10½" 36" ¾" 4¾" 22" 2¾"

4" 27½"

4½" rad

FRONT ELEVATION

Grain

16½" 16½"

5"

5½" 1½"

Castors 21"

END ELEVATION

57" Drawer stops

PLAN

FRONT

8½" 20½"

4⅛" rad

Leg 2¾"

1⅞"

Dovetail

Profile on edge of top

2¼"

1 inch SQUARES

36 inches 24 12 6 0

SCALE

Fig 1 Elevations, plan, and squared-off patterns for legs and columns; inset drawing shows moulding for edge of top.

strengthened by screwing on a metal strip shaped as in Fig 3 (D); this was commonly employed in tables of the period.

Legs

These are called 'claw' legs, and tripod tables fitted with them were often known as 'claw tables'. The squared-off drawing in Fig 1 shows the shape in side elevation, and also the taper in thickness from 1⅞in (48mm) to 1in (25mm); the toes of the legs finish square so that they can be fitted with socket castors.

It is essential that only sound and straight-grained wood is used for them, and because the splay makes the legs inherently liable to break it is important that the grain runs diagonally as shown by the arrow: you can economize on timber by nesting the template for one leg into another when marking out.

Frame

This is shown in Fig 2, and the construction is easy to follow. At the front, the two drawer rails (B) and (C) are dovetail-housed into the front corner blocks (A); while the back panel (Q), which is made up to match the front but is a dummy, is mortised and tenoned into the back corner blocks.

There are upper and lower end rails (H) and (M), both of which are also mortised and tenoned into the corner blocks; at the front the tenons have to be offset so that they do not foul the dovetail-housings. The upper and lower centre rails (E) and (F) are straightforward except that the latter also acts as a drawer runner and has two drawer guides (L) screwed and glued to it.

As already mentioned, the brackets (N) are hinged with knuckle joints; there are two infill pieces (P) and (T) at each end, the former being shaped as the reverse of the ogee curve on the bracket, plus a further infill panel (J). Parts (G) and (K) are the end drawer runners and guides respectively.

The transverse rail (D) runs the whole length of the frame and, as already mentioned, the columns are tenoned and wedged into it. The rail itself can be screwed into the rails (F), (G) and (M) from underneath.

The braces (R, see Fig 3 (B)) are quadrant-shaped and at one end can be either screwed and glued or mortised and tenoned to rail (D); the other end is tenoned into the circular column by means of a loose tenon as at Fig 3 (B). This end of each brace has to be hollowed out slightly to fit the curvature of the column and this can best be done with a half-round rasp or file. Once more, note the direction in which the grain should run – this is shown in the front elevation in Fig 1.

Drawers

Although the construction of these follows conventional methods (see Fig 3 (F)), there is a complication caused by having to fit the ebony beadings to the front, and the best way to tackle it is shown at Fig 3 (C). Small stringings are used along the bottom edges and the ends, but a beading covers the whole width of the top edge. As you can see, rebates are worked along the bottom and the end; but

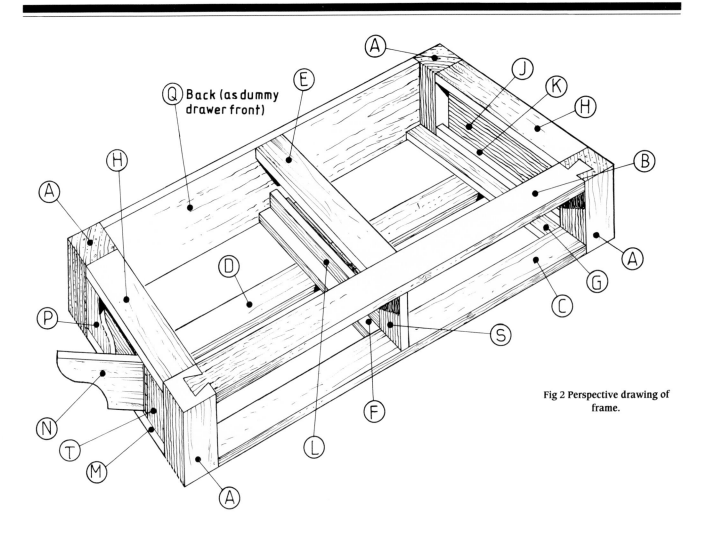

Q (Back (as dummy drawer front)

Fig 2 Perspective drawing of frame.

a mitre has to be cut away from part of the top beading to match the mitre on the end stringing.

The grain of the drawer bottom runs crosswise as shown at Fig 3 (F), and the bottom itself fits into grooves in the drawer sides and the back of the drawer front but is not glued; the drawer back is dovetailed in place so that it finishes just above the drawer bottom and the two are pinned (but not glued) together from underneath. The bottom should be made so that ¼in (6mm) or so protrudes at the back so that if shrinkage does take place it can be unpinned and pushed inward along the grooves and refixed.

Brasswork
This comprises four circular drawer knobs (two for the working drawer fronts, and two for the dummies), and four socket castors, all of which are readily obtainable.

Finish
This can be either a varnish or a wax finish, both of which are described in Appendix 5.

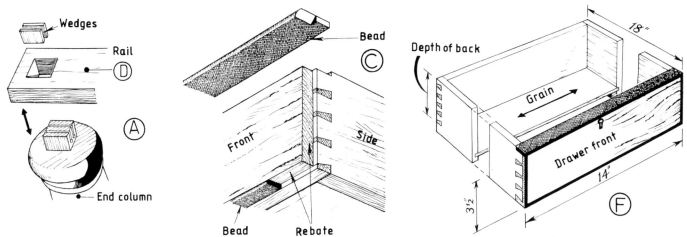

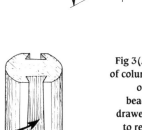

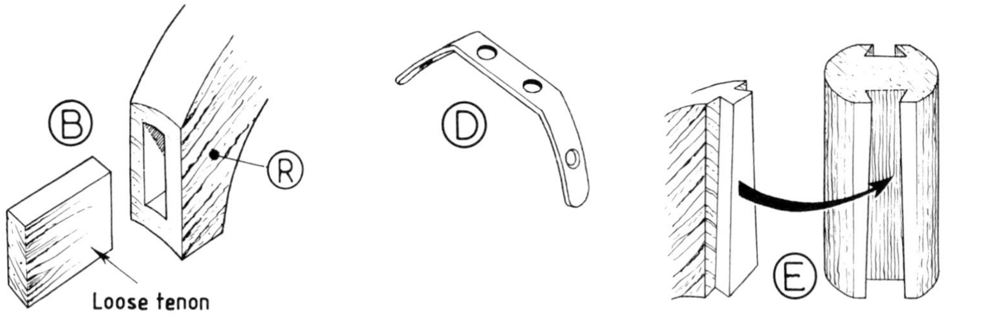

Fig 3(A) wedged tenon at top of column; (B) loose tenon used on brace; (C) fitting beading and stringing to drawer front; (D) metal plate to reinforce leg fixing; (E) details of slot dovetail joint; (F) details of drawer.

Cutting List

	inches			mm		
	L	W	T	L	W	T
1 top bed	23	37	¾	584	939	19
2 flaps, each	23	12	¾	584	305	19
2 end columns, each	18	3	2¾	457	76	70
4 legs (two from one piece)	21	11	1⅞	533	279	48
4 corner blocks (A), each	6	3	2¾	152	76	70
1 upper front rail (B)	34	3	¾	863	76	19
1 lower front rail (C)	33	3	¾	838	76	19
1 transverse rail (D)	37	3	¾	939	76	19
2 cross rails (E & F), each	18	3	¾	457	76	19
2 drawer runners (G), each	18	2	¾	457	51	19
2 upper end rails (H), each	18	3	¾	457	76	19
2 infill panels (J), each	16	4½	¾	407	115	19
2 drawer guides (K), each	18	1	¾	457	25	19
1 drawer guide (L)	18	1½	¾	457	38	19
2 lower end rails (M), each	17	3	¾	432	76	19
2 brackets (N), each	10	4½	¾	254	115	19
2 shaped pieces (P), each	9	4	¾	228	102	19
1 back panel (Q)	32	6	¾	812	152	19
2 braces (R), from one piece	7	7	¾	177	177	19
1 drawer division (S)	5	3	¾	127	76	19
2 filling pieces (T), each	4	2	¾	102	51	19
Drawers						
2 fronts, each	15	4	⅝	381	102	16
4 sides, each	19	4	½	482	102	13
2 backs, each	15	4	½	381	102	13
2 bottoms, each	14	19	¼	356	482	6
4 drawer stops from offcuts						
1 length of stringing, to cut all	264	⅛	1/16	6600	3	2
1 length of beading for top edges of drawers, to cut both	30	1	⅛	762	25	3

Generous working allowances have been made to lengths and widths; thicknesses are net.

CHEESE
COASTER

*A charming design that would grace
any dining table whether used to fulfil
its original function of circulating
cheese or dessert, or embellished with
flowers to act as a centrepiece.*

his kind of coaster was used to circulate the cheese round the dining table of many a country gentleman's home during the middle and late 18th century, and the design shown dates back to about 1780. With a little ingenuity it could be adapted to hold fruit, biscuits, or after-dinner mints. **Skill rating – 2.**

General remarks

As no large pieces of wood are needed it is practical to use solid mahogany as in the original piece. The construction is not difficult but does involve some simple steam bending, although even this could be avoided by altering the way the trough is made as described later.

Construction of the box

The lower part consists of a plain box which can be made with mitred corners reinforced by glued-in tongues as shown in Fig 1 (B). These tongues are best cut from 3mm or 4mm plywood, but if you have to use solid wood it is better to use cross-grained stuff as it will be less likely to split lengthwise.

Alternatively you could use the kind of secret mitred dovetails

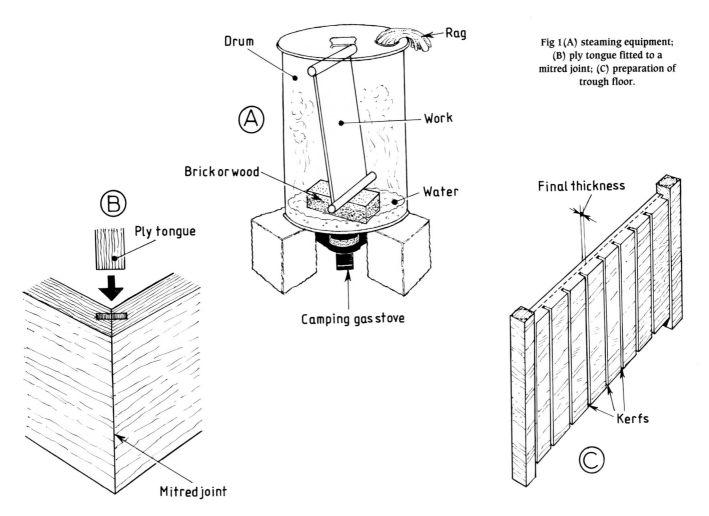

Fig 1 (A) steaming equipment; (B) ply tongue fitted to a mitred joint; (C) preparation of trough floor.

dealt with in Appendix 1, or if you have a biscuit jointer this is an ideal opportunity to put it to good use.

The original design runs on small brass castors fitted with leather wheels which are made by threading several leather discs on to the axles; but unfortunately these seem to be unobtainable. There are similar castors on the market but they are fitted with metal or porcelain wheels which would almost certainly scratch a polished surface.

A good alternative is to glue in a ½in (13mm) post in each corner so that its foot protrudes slightly and is shod with a small felt pad so that it does not scratch the table top; furthermore these posts strengthen the corners and also can be glued to the underside of the trough; see Fig 2(A).

Obviously the two longer sides of the box need to have their top edges sawn to fit under the trough floor and support it – a few glue blocks can be added for extra strength. One of the last jobs of all is to pin and glue the bottom of the box into a rebate worked on the lower edges and to notch it to fit round the corner posts; a small cockbeading is also pinned and glued on around the outside. If you decide to retain the bracket feet the easiest way is to cut and shape them from short lengths of ready-machined ogee moulding, mitring the corners and pinning and gluing them in place.

Making the trough

This is probably the trickiest but most interesting part of the job. Start by sawing the two sides to shape from the details shown in the squared-off drawing in Fig 2, not forgetting to saw out the central division as well.

The channels on the two sides are shallow, being only ⅛in (3mm) deep by ¼in (6mm) wide, and are best worked with a portable electric router; use a straight cutter fitted with a guide bush which can follow a hardboard template cut to shape and temporarily held down with double-sided tape. Note that holes have to be bored to accept the pins that are worked on the ends of the trough floor.

You will see from the photograph that the grain of the floor of the trough follows the serpentine shape and runs lengthwise, thus indicating that it must have been bent to shape. Start by preparing the blank which is shown in Fig 1(C) from a solid piece of mahogany; this finishes ⅞in (22mm) thick and can therefore come from 1in (25mm) stuff. Note that at each end a square piece is left which is later cut off to the finished width of 9in (229mm) while the remainder is reduced to a finished width of 8¼in (210mm). This enables you to spokeshave the ends together with the ⅜in (10mm) circular pins which fit the pre-bored holes in the trough sides.

There is still the matter of reducing the thickness of the remainder to ¼in (6mm) so that after bending, it will fit snugly into the channels on the sides. A good way to do this is to make a series of saw kerfs (either by hand or on a saw bench) ½in (13mm) deep and clear the waste away between them with a chisel; the final ⅛in (3mm) can then be removed with a router.

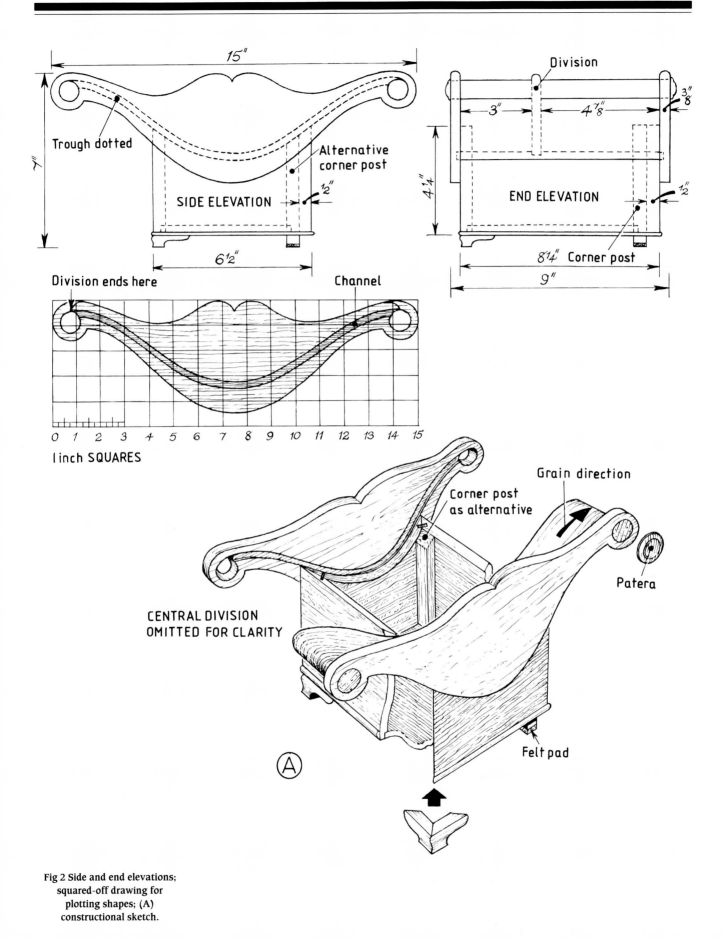

15"

Trough dotted

7"

SIDE ELEVATION

Alternative
corner post

½"

6½"

Division

3"   4⁷⁄₈"   ⅜"

4¼"

END ELEVATION

½"

8¼" Corner post

9"

Division ends here

Channel

0 1 2 3 4 5 6 7 8 9 10 11 12 13 14 15

1 inch SQUARES

Grain direction

Corner post
as alternative

Patera

CENTRAL DIVISION
OMITTED FOR CLARITY

Felt pad

Ⓐ

Fig 2 Side and end elevations;
   squared-off drawing for
   plotting shapes; (A)
   constructional sketch.

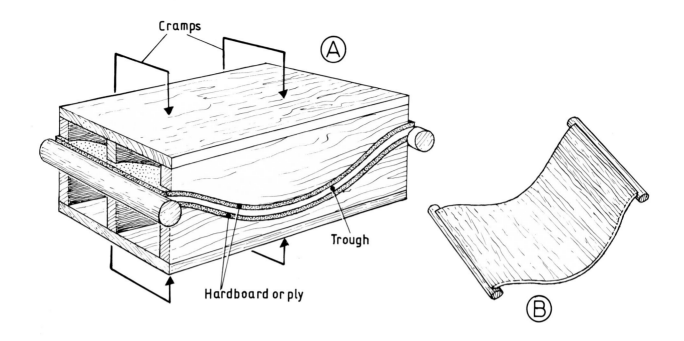

Cramps

(A)

Trough

Hardboard or ply

(B)

Fig 3(A) caul and cramp arrangement for bending the steamed trough floor; (B) alternative style for the trough floor using plywood.

Steam-bending the trough floor

Fig 1(A) shows the set-up for doing this which, although primitive, is effective for a one-off job. The drum will probably have previously contained oil or grease and will need to be thoroughly cleaned; it can be supported on concrete blocks or bricks and a camping gas stove placed underneath to supply the heat; the rag is a crude form of safety valve which will be blown out in the (very) unlikely event that excess pressure builds up. The work itself should not be allowed to touch the water and should be supported on a block of wood or something similar. Before starting to get up steam you will need to make the cauls illustrated in Fig 3(A) as they have to be ready as soon as the work comes out of the steaming drum.

The cauls could, of course, be made from solid pieces of softwood as they would have been in the old days when such pieces were not so expensive and difficult to come by. Those shown can be built up from pieces of, say, 1in (25mm) softwood nailed or screwed together with the meeting edges shaped rather more strongly than the curves of the channels on the trough sides. This is necessary because all timber springs back a little after it has been bent, the amount depending on its grain, seasoning, and other imponderables; it is therefore worthwhile to make the lowest point of the main curve about ⅜in (10mm) deeper and adjust the rest of the shape accordingly.

How long the trough floor will need to remain in the steam is also unpredictable, and the best plan is to leave it for half an hour or so and then try it; if it does not bend easily replace it and check it every fifteen minutes or so. When you do finally remove it, make sure that the cauls and the cramps (plus a helper) are near at hand so that no time is lost.

Once the trough floor has been housed and glued into the

channels and the pins fitted into the holes in the side, a few glue blocks can be added for extra strength. The central division can also be glued in place and fixed by means of small screws driven up from underneath; finally the paterae can be glued on and the bottom fixed to the box as mentioned above.

Alternative method

Fig 3 shows how a cross-grained piece of 4mm veneered plywood could be bent to the shape of the trough bottom without steaming; it would, of course, have to be slotted and glued into a separate cylindrical piece at each end. Although much simpler it would not, however, have the elegant appearance of the original.

Finish

As with most pieces of the period, the appropriate finish is the shellac varnish described in Appendix 5.

Cutting List

	inches			mm		
	L	W	T	L	W	T
1 trough bottom	17	9	¼	432	229	6
2 trough sides, each	16	5	⅜	407	127	10
1 central division	15	4	⅜	381	102	10
2 box sides, long, each	9	4¾	½	229	121	13
2 box sides, short, each	7	4¾	½	178	121	13
1 box bottom	7¾	5¾	⅜	197	146	10
4 corner posts, each	5¼	¾	½	133	19	13
Cockbeading, from 1 piece	31	¼	³⁄₁₆	787	6	5

Generous working allowances have been made to lengths and widths; thicknesses are net.

OAK GATE-LEG TABLE

So-called 'period' oak furniture is still widely, and often badly, made today and is frequently dismissed contemptuously as 'Jacobethan'. Our design from circa 1680 depicts an authentic and striking example of the true style.

This is an eye-catching design, not only because of the elegantly turned baluster legs and scroll feet but also because of the diagonal struts, which are most attractive and greatly increase the rigidity of the frame. The table probably dates back to about 1680 when it would have been described as a 'falling table' – the term 'gate-leg' was introduced during the 19th century. **Skill rating – 2.**

General remarks

The design is one which appears more suitable for making up in walnut rather than solid oak, but it is the latter timber that has been used. Because of their widths, the leaves are made up by rub-jointing long strips side by side (this technique is explained in Appendix 1). Either ash or a good-quality softwood would be a very acceptable substitute for oak.

Top and leaves

These are all ¾in (19mm) thick. When fully opened the top measures 54in by 36in (1371mm by 914mm), and in our design the dimensions of the bed and the ends have been slightly increased to give better stability.

Fig 3(A) gives a pattern for one half of a leaf drawn on a 1in (25mm) grid; the fully opened top is almost a regular ellipse except that the lower edges of the leaves are reduced by 1in (25mm) and rounded off as shown in the plan in Fig 1. The outer edges are finished with a thumb moulding (see Fig 3(F)), while a rule joint is employed on the hingeing edges.

Two stops, which can be either short lengths of dowel glued into shallow holes or small blocks screwed in place on the undersides of the leaves, prevent the gates from being opened too far, and are shown in the plan in Fig 1.

Turned parts

The patterns for the end columns (part K), the turned bottom stretcher (part G), and the foot of the gate-leg column (part M), are all shown in Fig 3 at (B), (C) and (D) respectively.

From Fig 3(B) you will see that each of the end columns has a tenon worked at top and bottom which is, of course, glued into place as described below. The turned sections of the four gate-leg columns (parts M and N) are exactly the same pattern as the end columns (part K), but the toes are turned as shown in Fig 3(D) and the small ears are glued on.

The bottom stretcher (part G) can (preferably) be turned as one piece but if your lathe bed is unable to accommodate it, you could turn a pin on each end of the turned section and glue them into the end squares.

Main frame

Fig 2 shows how this is assembled. The two end assemblies are the

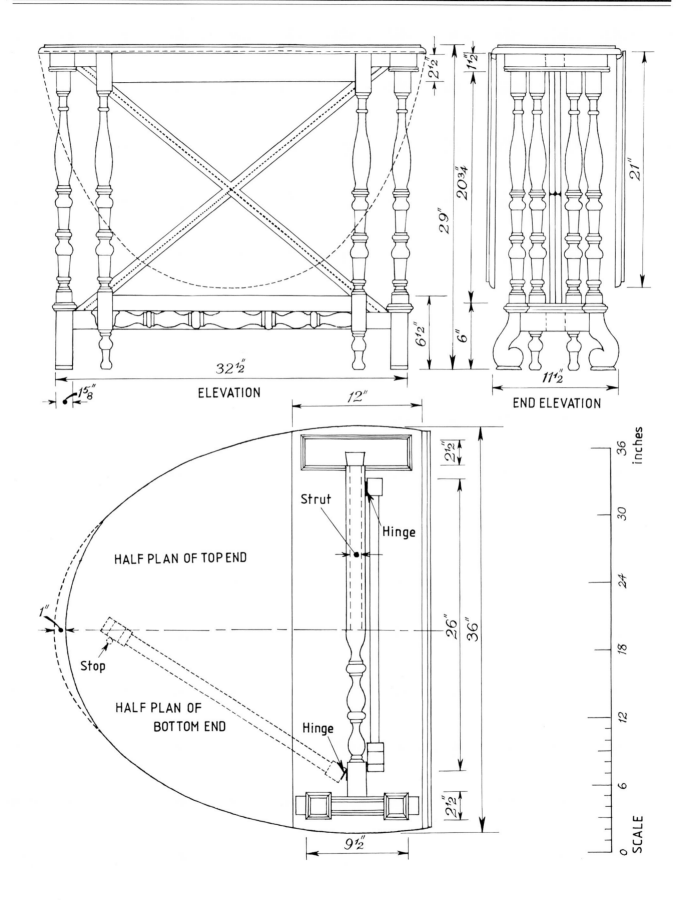

ELEVATION

END ELEVATION

HALF PLAN OF TOP END

HALF PLAN OF BOTTOM END

Strut

Hinge

Hinge

Stop

SCALE

inches

Fig 1 Elevations and plans

first to be dealt with, as their rigidity is essential to the whole table.

The feet can be made up by mortise and tenoning the scrolls (part F) to the blocks (part E) and if you can pin the tenons, so much the better; the pins could be driven in on the side which will face inwards when the job is assembled. An alternative and better method would be to join them by means of a dovetail halved joint similar to the one illustrated at the top left in Fig 2. Whichever way you do it, the facing pieces (part L) can be glued and pinned on to cover the joint – the tenons on the ends of the turned columns penetrate through them and help to fix them.

At the top, the tenons on the turned columns are glued into the block (part C), and then the small mouldings (part P) are pinned, glued, and mitred round them.

The next step is to join the two end sub-assemblies together by means of the upper stretcher (part D), the lower turned stretcher (G), and the diagonal struts (O). The best joint to use at the ends

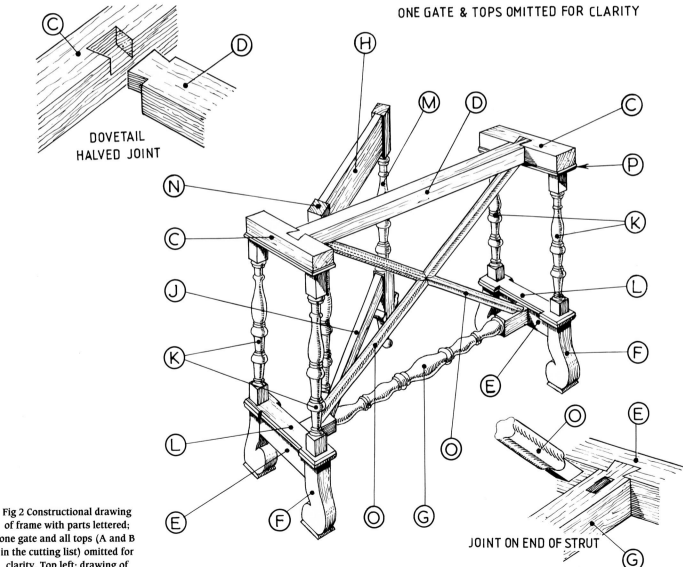

Fig 2 Constructional drawing of frame with parts lettered; one gate and all tops (A and B in the cutting list) omitted for clarity. Top left: drawing of dovetail halved joint; bottom right: joint at end of strut.

of both stretchers is the dovetail halved joint already referred to and shown in Fig 2 – in the case of the upper one the top bed will cover it, and the lower one will be hidden by the facing (part L).

Before working the diagonal struts and cutting the joints for them, it is essential to dry-assemble the frame so that you can measure their lengths accurately. The joint used at each end is shown at the lower right of Fig 2 and consists of a sloping tenon which enters a slanted mortise.

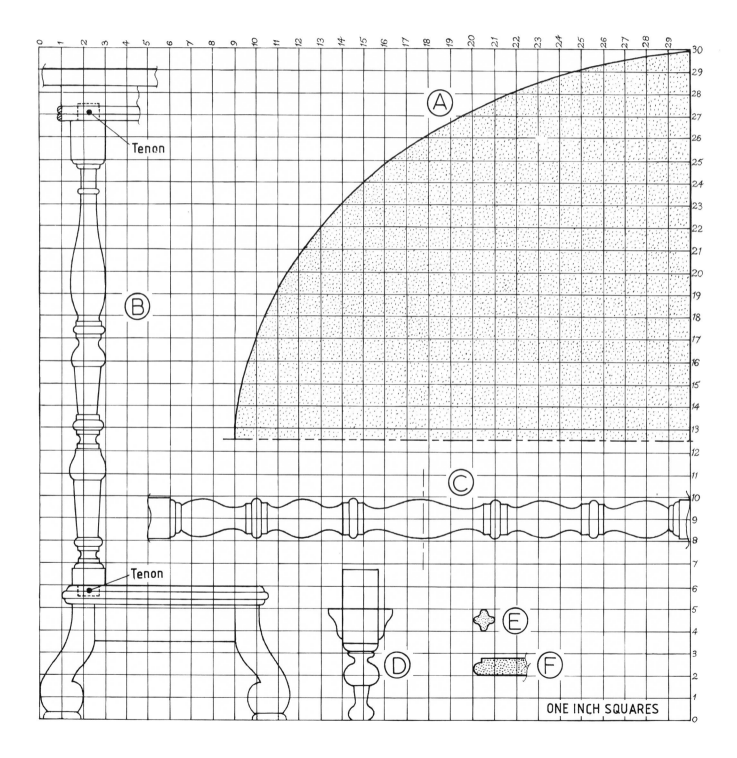

ONE INCH SQUARES

Gate-leg frames

These are straightforward frames with the rails mortised and tenoned into the squares on the columns (parts M and N). On the table in the photograph the tenons are through tenons – in other words, they penetrate right through the squares – but this is not obligatory unless you require historical authenticity.

The frames are hinged at top and bottom to parts (D) and (G) respectively with wrought-iron backflaps (brass-finish hinges would be out of place and, even if you are not concerned with historical accuracy, it still looks better if steel hinges are used).

Fixing the top bed and leaves

As the top bed is solid, it is essential that the method employed for fixing it should allow for any shrinkage that will almost certainly occur, and this means using either buttoning or shrinkage plates. Both features are explained and illustrated in Appendix 1.

The leaves are rule-jointed to the bed, a process also fully described in Appendix 1.

Finish

The most suitable (and historically accurate) finish is a wax one which can be re-applied from time to time. For details of this finish see Appendix 5.

Cutting List

Fig 3 One-inch squared-off drawing giving patterns for (A) half-plan of leaf; (B) turned part of end columns and gate-legs; (C) turned part of lower stretcher; (D) toe on end of gate-leg; (E) section of strut; (F) profile of top edge moulding.

	inches			mm		
	L	W	T	L	W	T
1 top bed (A)	38	13	¾	965	330	19
2 leaves (B), each	38	22	¾	965	559	19
2 end blocks (C), each	10½	3	1½	267	76	35
1 upper stretcher rail (D)	33	2½	1⅛	838	64	29
2 feet blocks (E), each	8½	2	1⅝	216	51	42
4 scrolled feet (F), each	6	3	1⅝	153	76	42
1 lower stretcher rail (G)	33	2½	1¾	838	64	45
2 gate upper rails (H), each	25	3	⅞	635	76	23
2 gate lower rails (J), each	25	2	⅞	635	51	23
4 legs (K), each	24	2¼	1⅝	609	58	42
2 facings (L), each	11	3	⅞	279	76	23
2 gate outer legs (M), each	30	2¼	1⅝	762	58	42
2 gate inner legs (N), each	30	2¼	1⅝	762	58	42
2 struts (O), each	39	1½	1	990	35	25
Moulding for blocks (C), total length	54	½	¼	1371	13	6
4 ears from offcuts						

Generous working allowances have been made to lengths and widths; thicknesses are net.

GOTHIC-STYLE ELBOW CHAIR

A sturdy no-nonsense chair incorporating the Gothic style splad frequently used by Thomas Chippendale. Similar designs are often found in country manor houses and date back to the second half of the 18th century.

The Gothic style was one of the longest lived in the history of furniture and in one form or another was popular from the early part of the 18th century until the middle of the 19th. Thomas Chippendale used it in many of his designs, and on Plate XVI in the third edition of his book *The Gentleman and Cabinet-Maker's Director* published in 1762, the central design for a chair back is very similar to that on the chair illustrated here, which was made about 1765. **Skill rating – 3.**

General description

This is a graceful chair and despite its light appearance is very strong as the frame is strengthened by a sturdy underframe of stretcher rails and also by seat brackets. The toe-in of the backfeet gives a pleasing look to the back without the need to curve them and thereby waste wood. The arms are set at an angle on the side seat rails so that the chair seems to invite one to sit down.

It must be stressed that working the shaped parts can only be done with either a bandsaw or a bowsaw (shown in Fig 3(C)); the latter is also known as a 'chairmaker's saw' or a 'Betty saw', and although at one time it fell into disuse it is now readily available.

Backfeet

These are shown in the elevations in Fig 1 and you should be able to plot the shape from the squared-off drawings, which are sub-divided into 2in (51mm) squares, and then nest one backfoot into the other when marking them out.

Once they have been cut out on the bandsaw or by a bowsaw it is advisable to chop out the various mortises before rounding them off; this rounding off (called 'benching' in the trade) is best done by hand with a spokeshave, starting about $1\frac{3}{4}$in (45mm) above the seat rail as shown in the side elevation, Fig 1.

Although the backfeet toe in, the mortises for the side seat rails and the side stretcher rails are nevertheless made with their walls parallel to the sides of the backfeet, and the tenons on the rails are angled slightly to fit them, as described later. The exception is in the case of the rear stretcher rail, where the mortise has to be vertical as shown in the side elevation, Fig 1.

As you can see from Fig 2(B), the arms are notched around the backfeet and it is better to do this once the complete frame has been test-fitted together dry – that is, without glue. You will then be able to judge more accurately where the notches need to be so that the arms are level.

Seat frame and underframe

As the front legs are square and straight, cramping up the frame should present no difficulty. There are, however, two joints which may cause problems, and the first is the one already referred to which consists of angling the tenons on the side seat rails to enter the mortises on the backfeet.

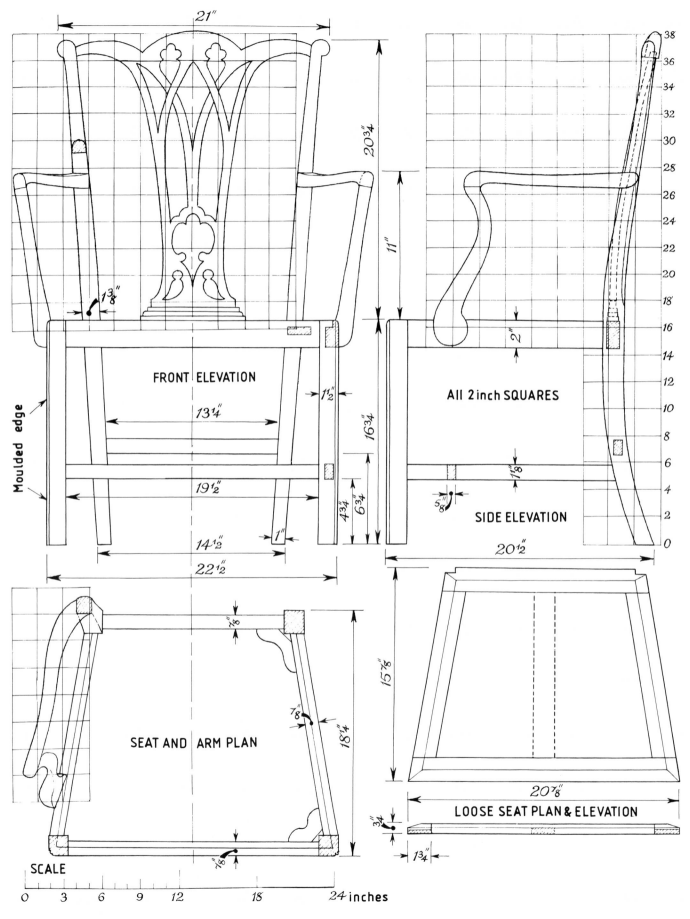

FRONT ELEVATION

Moulded edge

SIDE ELEVATION

All 2 inch SQUARES

SEAT AND ARM PLAN

LOOSE SEAT PLAN & ELEVATION

SCALE

0   3   6   9   12   18   24 inches

Fig 1 Elevations and plan; also
elevation and plan of loose
seat frame.

Fig 3(A) shows details of this, and you will see that the tenons are first cut oversize so that you can chisel the sides at an angle as at Fig 2(B); it may also be necessary to do the same at the top and bottom of the tenons.

The other tricky joint is the one illustrated at Fig 2 (C), where the side seat rail meets the front leg at an angle which necessitates cutting the tenon to accommodate it.

A rebate ⅜in by ⅜in (10mm by 10mm) is worked on the inside edges of the front and side seat rails, but not on the back one; you will have to carry the rebate on to the top squares of the front legs by chopping out the inner corners with a mortise chisel. This rebate supports the loose drop-in seat; although the overall thickness of the frame is ¾in (19mm), the outer edges are bevelled off as in the elevation in Fig 1. The four seat brackets can be glued and screwed in place so that their top faces are flush with the rebates and thereby give extra support to the loose seat frame, as well as generally strengthening the whole of the chair frame.

The underframe stretcher rails are fixed with straightforward mortise and tenon joints, and the only point to note is that the shoulders of the tenons where the side stretchers meet the backfeet need to be cut at an angle as shown in the side elevation in Fig 1.

The splad

Probably the most difficult part of the chair to make, the curved shape of this can best be cut out with a bowsaw which needs to have at least a 14in (356mm) blade. The job could be done on a bandsaw but very few such machines allow the saw guides to be lifted up far enough to enable the wood blank to be sawn while standing on edge. Whichever you use, it will make things much easier if you first make some shallow transverse sawcuts as shown in Fig 3(B). If neither of these methods is feasible, the job can be done using wide chisels, rasps or small planes and the transverse sawcuts will still prove helpful.

Having completed this, the next step is to saw along the dotted outlines as in Fig 3(B) to give you the general splad shape, but before starting to cut out the pierced apertures it is advisable to work the tenons at top and bottom. They are quite small as the finished thickness of the splad is ⁷⁄₁₆in (11mm) and they need be only about ½in (13mm) long with ¹⁄₁₆in (1.6mm) shoulders.

The splad is now ready for the pierced apertures to be cut out. The best tool is either a fretsaw or a coping saw; although a power jigsaw could be used, it might prove too fierce to saw out the more delicate parts.

A point to bear in mind is that splads like this should not be glued into the shoe on the back seat rail but should be a snug, dry fit to allow any movement of the timber to take place without splitting. To make the job easier, the shoe consists of two long and two short pieces of moulding which fit around the tenon on the splad, being mitred at the corners and pinned and glued in position. You will need to cut mortises on the crest (top) rail to accept the tenons on the upper end of the splad.

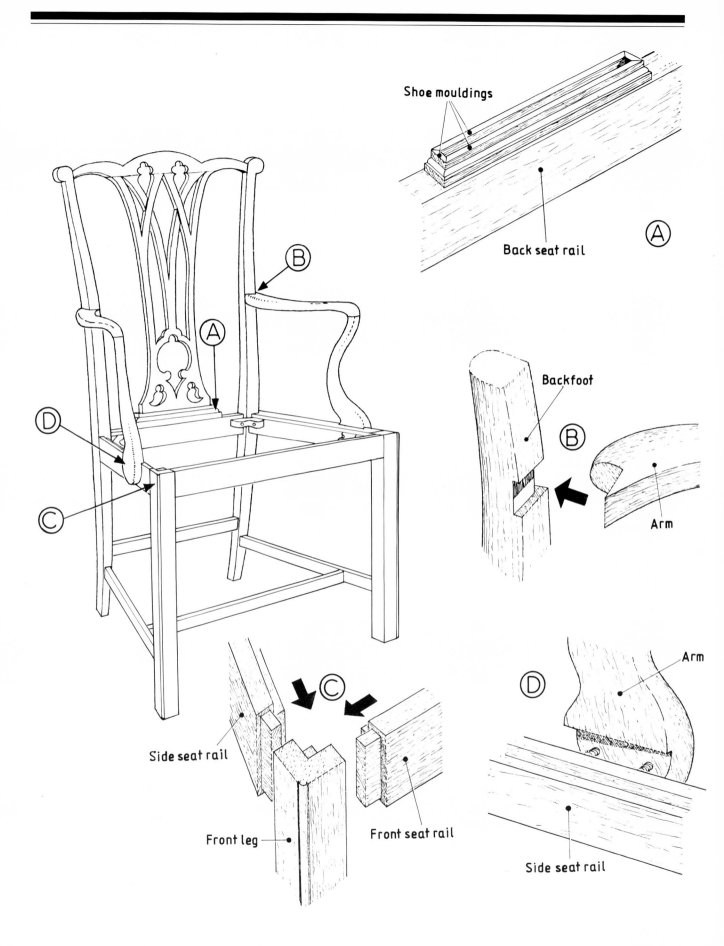

Shoe mouldings

Back seat rail

(A)

Backfoot

(B)

Arm

Side seat rail

(C)

Front leg

Front seat rail

(D)

Arm

Side seat rail

Fig 2(A) how shoe mouldings are arranged; (B) fitting an arm to a backfoot; (C) the joint between the front leg and the side seat rail; (D) how the stump is fitted.

Crest (or top) rail

This is slightly dished by ½in (13mm) in its length and again it will need to be sawn out to shape with a bowsaw or a bandsaw; the important thing is to mark and chop out the mortises for the splad and make the tenons which enter mortises in the backfeet before attempting to saw out the shape. It is much easier to do this kind of work while the wood is still square and flat.

Arm and stump

The sizes and shapes of these are shown in the elevations and plan in Fig 1, and once more you will need a bowsaw or a bandsaw to cut out the rough shapes, remembering to allow an extra ½in (13mm) on the top of the stump to allow for the tenon that enters the arm.

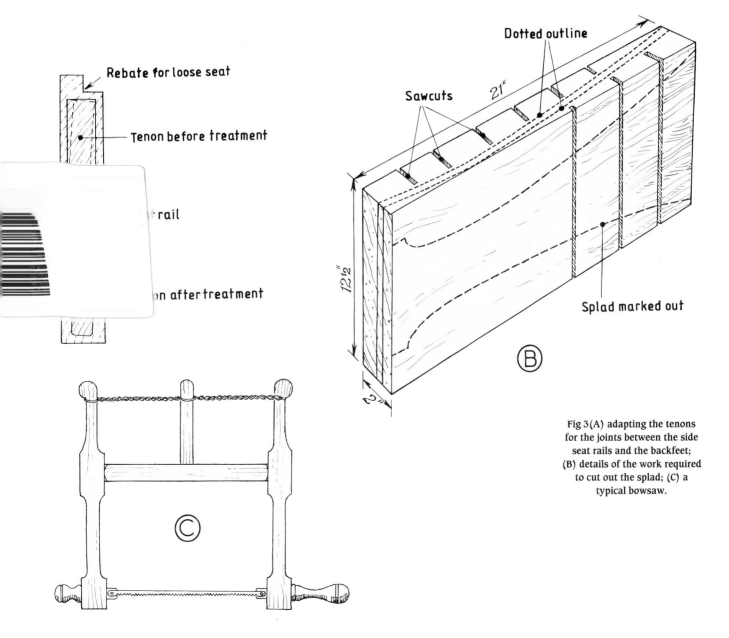

Fig 3(A) adapting the tenons for the joints between the side seat rails and the backfeet; (B) details of the work required to cut out the splad; (C) a typical bowsaw.

As you can see from Fig 1 and Fig 2(D), the arm stump is fixed to the side seat rail at an angle, so imparting a pleasing splayed effect to the arms. The fixing can be by means of glue and screws driven through from the outside, with their heads pelleted (see Appendix 1).

Fig 2(B) illustrates how the arms fit into notches cut in the backfeet, and the joint should be further strengthened by inserting dowels and gluing up. By far the best plan is to fix the arms and stumps into final position before rounding them off with a spokeshave.

This rounding off, or benching, is a matter of personal taste and can only be done by eye – in fact, if done well, it is one of the marks of a good chairmaker. The same remarks apply to benching the backfeet and the edges and the front face of the crest rail.

Loose drop-in seat

Beech is the best wood to use for making this as it is strong and close-grained and will accept tacks without splitting. Halved joints can be used for the corners, reinforced with screws and glue, and as already mentioned, the upper edges are bevelled. Note that the overall sizes are ⅛in (3mm) smaller all round than the frame into which it fits, so allowing for the thickness of the cover. The central rail shown dotted in the plan and elevation in Fig 1 is generally found only in modern designs and gives added strength. To be true to period the seat should be stuffed with horse hair, but details of alternative more modern materials and methods are described in Appendix 6.

Finish

Chairs tend to be subjected to harsher usage than most pieces of furniture, and consequently a hard varnish finish would be the best choice as described in Appendix 5.

Cutting List

	inches			mm		
	L	W	T	L	W	T
2 backfeet, from one piece	39	6½	2	990	165	51
2 arms, from one piece	16	4½	1¼	407	115	32
2 arm stumps, from one piece	14	6½	1½	356	165	38
1 splad	21	12½	7/16	533	318	11
2 front legs, each	17½	1¾	1½	445	45	38
1 front seat rail	22½	2¼	7/8	572	58	23
2 side seat rails, each	17½	2¼	7/8	445	58	23
1 back seat rail	17	2¼	7/8	432	58	23
1 crest (top) rail	21	3	1¾	533	76	45
1 front stretcher rail	21	1½	5/8	533	38	16
1 intermediate stretcher rail	21½	1½	5/8	546	38	16
1 back stretcher rail	14¾	1½	5/8	375	38	16
2 side stretcher rails, each	18	1½	5/8	457	38	16
4 brackets, each	5	2	½	127	51	13
Loose seat						
1 front rail	22	2	¾	559	51	19
1 back rail	17	2	¾	432	51	19
2 side rails	17½	2	¾	445	51	19
1 central rail (optional)	17	2	¾	432	51	19
Shoe mouldings						
2 long pieces	8½	1¼	¾	216	32	19
2 short pieces	1½	1¼	¾	38	32	19

Generous working allowances have been made to lengths and widths; thicknesses are net.

PEMBROKE
TABLE

Another perennial favourite, the Pembroke table has appeared in several guises during the last two centuries — some good, and some bad. Our example is an authentic piece from about 1790.

Although Sheraton in his *Cabinet Dictionary* (1803) wrote that the name of the table was derived from that of the lady who first ordered one, it is just as likely that the design was originally made for Henry Herbert, Earl of Pembroke, who was known as 'the architect earl' because of his enthusiasm for building. The name was sometimes spelt 'Pembrook', and the design was also referred to as a 'universal table' which allows sofa tables to be members of the family.

Our example, in mahogany from circa 1790, has semicircular flaps which are supported by hinged brackets; the edges of the flaps are crossbanded with tulipwood veneer, and one end of the framing contains a drawer while the other is made as a dummy drawer front. **Skill rating – 3.**

Top

This consists of the two flaps and the centre bed to which they are hinged by means of rule joints (described in Appendix 1). This kind of joint involves working a half-round on the two long edges of the bed which mate with concave mouldings on the straight edges of the flaps, and this can best be done using solid timber. It follows, then, that the bed and flaps will need to be built up from boards rub-jointed together edge-to-edge as described in Appendix 1.

The semicircular edges of the flaps are not moulded but left square, and a shallow depression needs to be scratched or routed to accept the tulipwood crossbanding; the depth of the depression depends upon the thickness of the veneer.

The top, when fully opened out, is not a perfect ellipse but is slightly flattened where it approaches the parallel with the major axis – the squared-off drawing at Fig 1 (A) will help you to achieve the correct shape. For historical authenticity the top should be pocket-screwed to the frame.

Legs

These are the plain square tapered Marlboro' pattern with the taper beginning from the point as shown at Fig 2 (D); there are no spade toes to worry about as the feet fit into 1in (25mm) square socket castors.

All corners of the legs have small ⅛in (3mm) square stringings let into them. On the original design no doubt these were long narrow strips cut from a sheet of veneer which would itself have been the requisite thickness, but you will probably have to either buy them in or make them up yourself.

There remains the job of working the recesses on the corners of the legs to accept these stringings, plus that of wasting away the groundwork for the inlaid patterns on the faces; see Fig 2 (D). This procedure should not prove to be too difficult especially if you hold each of the legs in turn in the jig which is described later in Appendix 1, Joints and Cabinet Work.

Fig 1 Elevations and plan: (A) squared-off plan of half of the top; (B) detail of banding; (C) corner of frame.

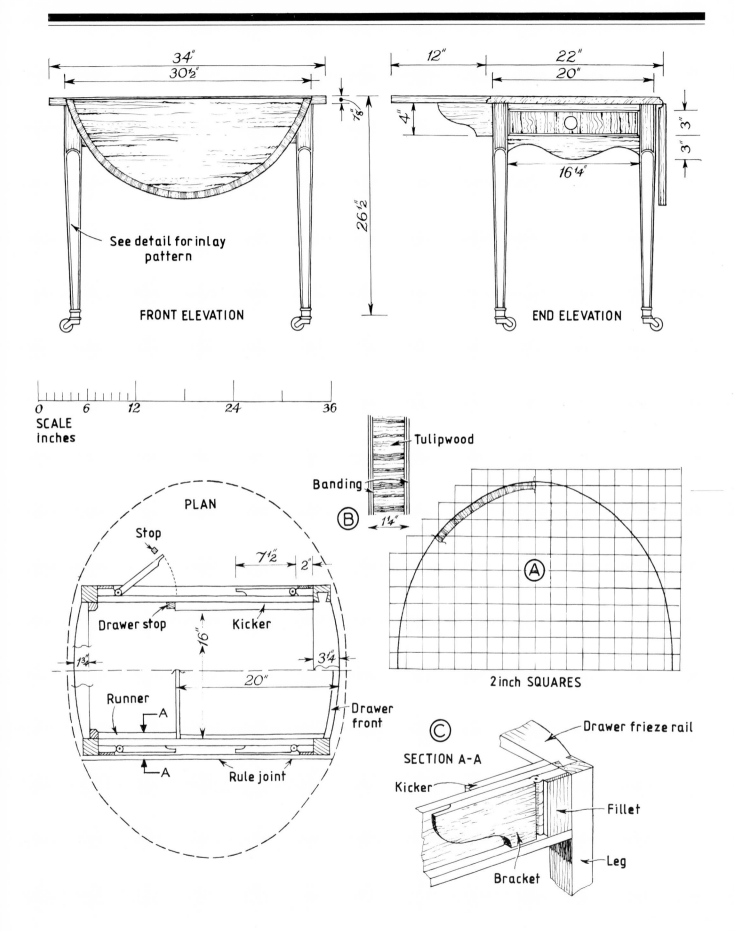

FRONT ELEVATION

See detail for inlay pattern

END ELEVATION

SCALE inches

PLAN

Stop

Drawer stop

Kicker

Runner

Drawer front

Rule joint

Tulipwood

Banding

Ⓑ

Ⓐ

2 inch SQUARES

Ⓒ

SECTION A-A

Drawer frieze rail

Kicker

Fillet

Leg

Bracket

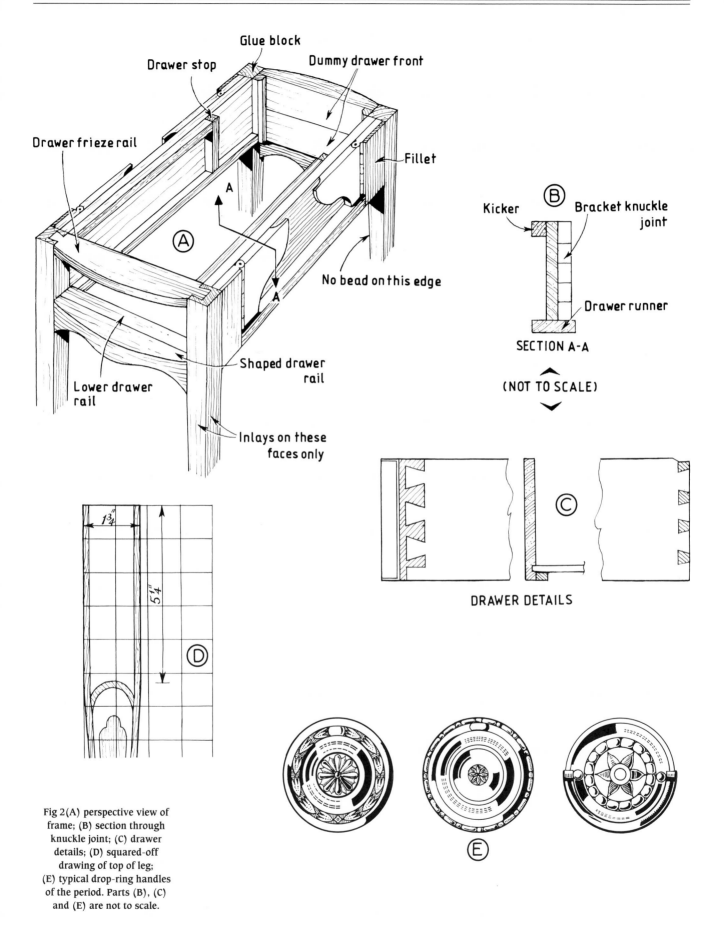

Glue block

Drawer stop

Dummy drawer front

Drawer frieze rail

Fillet

Kicker

Bracket knuckle joint

Drawer runner

SECTION A-A

(NOT TO SCALE)

No bead on this edge

Shaped drawer rail

Lower drawer rail

Inlays on these faces only

DRAWER DETAILS

$1\frac{3}{4}"$

$5\frac{1}{4}"$

Fig 2(A) perspective view of frame; (B) section through knuckle joint; (C) drawer details; (D) squared-off drawing of top of leg; (E) typical drop-ring handles of the period. Parts (B), (C) and (E) are not to scale.

Frame

This is shown in plan in Fig 1 and in perspective at Fig 2(A), the rails and brackets being ¾in (19mm) finished thickness. The drawer frieze rail is lap-dovetailed into the legs, while the dummy drawer front at the other end is mortise and tenoned into them – this piece can be built up from two pieces glued edge to edge. Similarly, the shaped piece on the front of the drawer rail is glued and tongued to the piece behind it; all these features are shown in Figs 1 and 2(A).

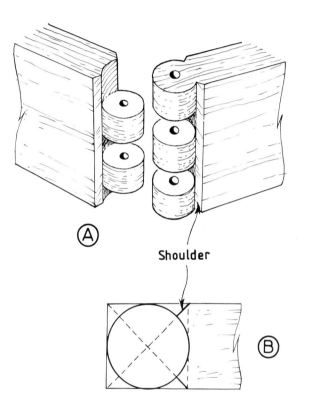

Fig 3 (A) sketch of knuckle joint; (B) plan showing how shoulders are plotted.

There are four fillets – one at each corner – which are glued and pinned to the faces of the brackets for the sake of appearance. Each of the four brackets is hinged by means of a knuckle joint, details of which are shown in Fig 3. It is one of the trickiest joints to make but is certainly one of the strongest; it can only succeed if a close-grained hardwood such as beech is employed to minimize wear.

Fig 3(B) shows how to mark out the circle and the shoulders in plan and it's obvious that marking out has to be really precise for the joint to function properly. Use a dovetail saw and a chisel for cutting and shaping the shoulders and also for the horizontal cuts of the knuckles as the saw teeth have no set and therefore give a fine cut which should, nevertheless, always be on the waste side of the line. Rounding off the knuckles is a laborious job – you will probably have to saw off the corners first and then use a shoulder plane, and a rasp or file or both, to accomplish the final shaping. A coping saw is handy for cutting out the sockets but there is no easy way of shaping the concave recesses other than to use a very sharp chisel followed by glasspaper wrapped around a rubber made to match the concavity. The whole joint is held together with a metal pin about $^3/_{16}$in (5mm) diameter; generally a large nail does the job perfectly.

Drawer

Usually these tables were fitted with one drawer, as in our example, but occasionally you will find one with two. Details are given in the plan in Fig 1 and at Fig 2(C); note also the arrangement of the kickers and runners shown in the plan in Fig 1.

Handles

As with the serpentine-fronted sideboard (pages 53–60), these are easily obtainable from several of the suppliers listed on page 158, and the socket castors are equally readily available. For your guidance Fig 2(E) shows three typical patterns of handles of the period.

Finish

To be historically accurate this should be the shellac-based varnish described in Appendix 5.

Cutting List

	inches			mm		
	L	W	T	L	W	T
1 top bed	36	24	$^7/_8$	915	610	22
2 top leaves, each	32	14	$^7/_8$	813	356	22
4 legs, each	28	2	$1^3/_4$	711	51	45
2 side frame rails, each	28	$4^1/_2$	$^3/_4$	711	115	19
2 pcs for dummy drawer front, each	19	$2^1/_2$	$^3/_4$	482	64	19
2 pcs, shaped, for drawer fronts, each	19	$3^1/_2$	$1^3/_4$	482	89	45
1 drawer frieze rail	19	4	$^3/_4$	482	102	19
1 lower drawer rail	19	2	$^3/_4$	482	51	19
2 drawer runners, each	28	$3^1/_2$	$^3/_4$	711	89	19
2 drawer kickers, each	21	$1^1/_4$	$^7/_8$	533	32	22
2 drawer stops, each	4	$1^1/_4$	$^7/_8$	102	32	22
4 fillets, each	$4^1/_2$	$2^1/_2$	$^3/_8$	115	64	10
4 brackets, each	10	$4^1/_2$	$^3/_4$	254	115	19
1 shaped drawer front, from	17	$3^1/_2$	$2^1/_2$	432	89	64
2 drawer sides, each	$19^1/_2$	$3^1/_2$	$^3/_8$	495	89	10
1 drawer back	17	$3^1/_2$	$^3/_8$	432	89	10
1 drawer bottom	$19^1/_2$	17	$^1/_4$	495	432	6

Generous working allowances have been made to lengths and widths; thicknesses are net.

SIDEBOARD WITH SERPENTINE FRONT

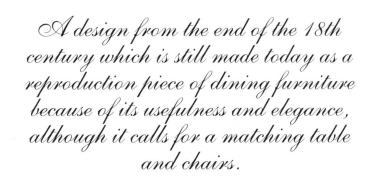

A design from the end of the 18th century which is still made today as a reproduction piece of dining furniture because of its usefulness and elegance, although it calls for a matching table and chairs.

Photograph courtesy of Sotheby's ©

A typical sideboard of the late 18th century dated at about 1785; it is in mahogany, and has spade-toe legs. The central drawer is flanked by two deep drawers; the latter had storage for table linen and cutlery, and were often fitted with cellarets for holding bottles and sometimes lead-lined sinks for rinsing glasses. The front is laid with figured mahogany veneers and decorated with inlaid oval fans on the legs and fan corners in the spandrels of the apron. **Skill rating – 4.**

Top: traditional construction

This is comparatively thick at 1⅛in (29mm), which means that those who want to make an authentic copy will need to start with 1¼in (32mm) solid mahogany and plane it down. Alternatively, if the top is to be veneered the main part could be thinner, say ¾in (19mm), and lining pieces 1in (25mm) wide by 1⅛in (29mm) thick could be tongued to the edges all round, thus forming the overhang. In order to achieve the depth of the top (28in or 711mm) several pieces will need to be rub-jointed edge to edge whether the top is to be veneered or not. (This jointing method is described in Appendix 1.)

If solid mahogany is not being used then any alternative timber has to be primarily suitable as a groundwork for the veneer. In the old days some makers used solid Honduras mahogany and veneered it; or oak which had to be quarter-sawn to be reasonably stable. Unfortunately this method of sawing exposes the medullary rays which are harder than the rest of the wood and do not accept glue to the same extent, with the result that over the years the veneer tends to lift.

Probably the best alternative is Canadian yellow pine although it is scarce; others are poplar, sweet chestnut, or Parana pine, and whichever is chosen must be carefully selected and thoroughly seasoned to the correct moisture content of about 8 per cent.

The edges of the top are faced with cross-grained veneers and a black stringing is let in and glued around the arrises to protect the edges of the veneers. As is well known, veneers of the period were much thicker than their modern equivalents, up to ⅛in (3mm) thick, and the stringing would have been laid in the gap where the one on the top met the one on the edge.

A modern thin cross-grained veneer laid on the edges will make it easier to negotiate the rounded corners although it is likely to split; however, any splits invariably follow the grain and are invisible once the veneer is laid. Those who have any qualms can lay a second strip on top of the first to ensure that there are no unsightly gaps.

Legs

Fig 1(B), (C), and (D) illustrate how to machine these on an overhand planer; note that the drawings are diagrammatic only, as guards must be in place and push sticks used to put the work

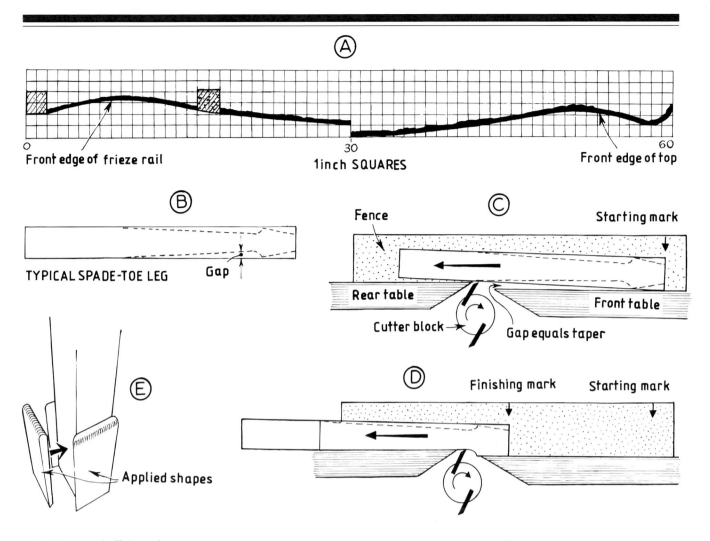

Fig 1 (A) squared-off plans of the front edges; (B) typical spade-toe leg; (C) and (D) method of working a leg on an overhand planer; (E) building up a toe.

through. The important features are that the tables are set to differ in height by an amount corresponding to the gap at (B); and the cutting periphery of the planer knives creates the curve above the spade toe.

Note that when the wood is lowered on to the knives to begin the cut a small ridge results which has to be planed off by hand afterwards; this means that it is necessary to make an allowance for this when applying the starting mark to the fence.

The same technique can be employed for a tapered leg that has no toe but there is a hidden danger, namely that the top end of the leg must lap over the edge of the rear table by ¼in (6mm) or so before starting the cut otherwise it could drop in the gap between the tables and kick back violently.

Carcase

This sideboard has all four front legs in the same plane and set square to the front and back – in more expensive designs the legs are often set at an angle to follow the curve of the top so that the whole front presents an unbroken shape, but this can complicate framing up the drawers. In our case, however, the work is made easier because the framing is square throughout and so lends itself readily to straightforward drawer making, joint cutting, and cramping up.

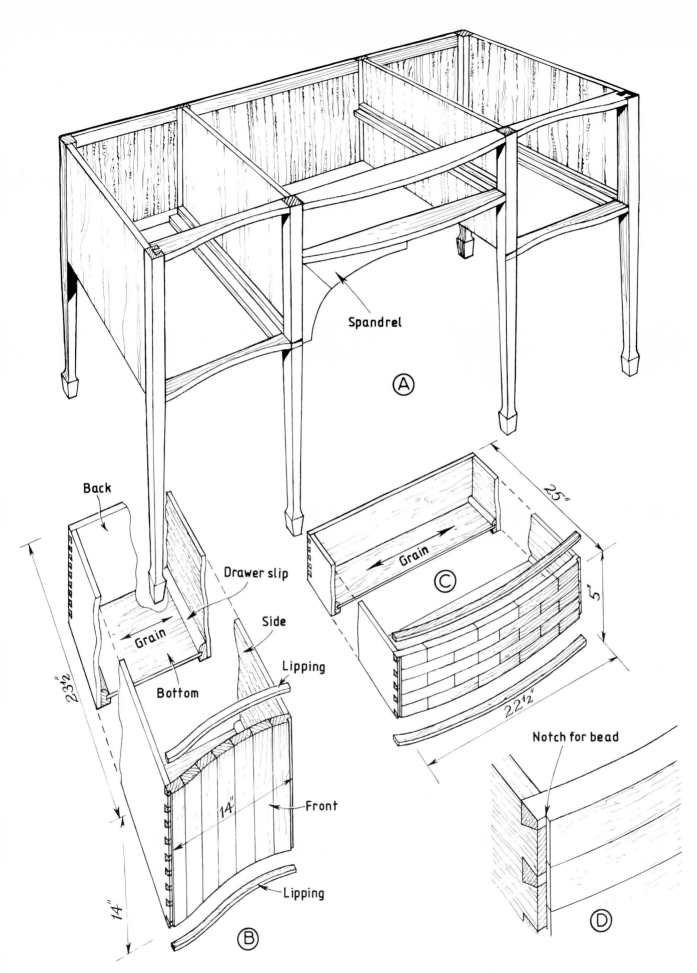

Spandrel

Back

Drawer slip

Side

Grain

Bottom

Lipping

23½"

14"

14"

Front

Lipping

Ⓐ

Ⓑ

Grain

25"

5"

22½"

Ⓒ

Notch for bead

Ⓓ

56

Fig 2 (A) perspective view of frame; (B) details of large drawer; (C) small drawer; (D) detail of corner of drawer front.

The joints on the carcase frame are all orthodox and what one would expect to find. The panels in the ends and the central divisions could be ½in (13mm) solid mahogany, although ⅜in (10mm) veneered ply would be even better as it is available with a straight-grained mahogany veneer on the exterior and a compensating veneer (often called a 'balancer') on the reverse and so is free from any tendency to shrink.

Back

In many examples of antique case furniture like desks, bureaux and sideboards the backs consisted of boards of solid timber such as oak or pine simply nailed in place; they were frequently quite crudely finished and showed saw marks, which is understandable when one appreciates the labour involved in pit-sawing comparatively thin boards.

Because of the needs of timber conservation our design has been given a panelled back. This involves inserting two muntins, one at each side of the central section; the outer panels could be ⅜in (10mm) veneered ply but the central panel should be thicker – ⅝in (16mm) veneered ply or veneered medium density fibre board (MDF) for example, so that the bottom edge will not need a rail and the drawer runners and guides can be fixed directly to it.

Drawers and apron

Appendix 1 gives details of standard practice for making drawer framing and both the two deep drawers and the central drawer follow this. The fronts of the two deep drawers are built up by the coopering method but the central drawer front uses 'brick' construction, and both are shown in Fig 2 (B) and (C). Note, however, that as the curve on the central drawer front is only shallow there is the alternative that it could be cut from one solid piece, or from two pieces glued together. With the brick construction, moreover, there is the added complication of cutting a notch on the vertical edges to accept a beading which is the same thickness (but narrower in width) than the lippings on the upper and lower edges, as shown in Fig 2 (D).

It was common for the drawer stuff, consisting of the sides, end and bottom, to have been oak although good quality, knot-free pine was also used. The grain of the drawer bottom should run from side to side as this was a characteristic of drawers made from about 1740 onwards and ied to the bottom being inserted loose (without glue) into the drawer slips shown in Fig 2 (B) and (C). The front end should be located (again, no glue) into a groove worked on the inside of the drawer front; at the other end it should run underneath the bottom edge of the back to which it is pinned but not glued. These precautions are needed to accommodate any shrinkage of the drawer bottom, and some makers allowed the bottom to protrude ¼in (6mm) or so beyond the back so that the pins could be removed if the bottom had to be pushed forward to take up any shrinkage.

George Hepplewhite, in his *Cabinet Maker and Upholsterer's Guide* gives the following description of the interior fittings of the drawers in a sideboard similar to ours:

> … the right hand drawer has partitions for nine bottles. … the partition is one inch and a half from the bottom, behind this is a place for cloths or napkins the whole depth of the drawer. The drawer on the left has two divisions, the hinder one lined with green cloth to hold plate etc under a cover; the front one is lined with lead for the convenience of holding water to wash glasses etc. … there must be a valve-cock or plug at the bottom, to let off the dirty water; and also in the other drawer, to change the water necessary to keep the wine etc cool; or they may be made to take out. The long drawer in the middle is adapted for the table linen etc.

The washing-up cistern could be utilized in a modern design to hold ice and would certainly not be lead but probably plastic; the remaining features could well be incorporated as they are.

Top: construction using modern materials

This section is for those who are not primarily concerned with authenticity and who, of necessity or by design, want to avail themselves of modern materials which are easily obtainable and predictable in their behaviour.

For them, the top can be ¾in (19mm) thick MDF on which the mahogany veneer can be laid. As MDF is supplied in large sheets the top can be a slab cut to size; although not essential it is advisable to lay a counter veneer on the underside to prevent the pull of the glue on the face veneer from causing the MDF to bow.

The next step is to prepare a straight-grained lipping which can be tongued to the edges of the top; this could be 1⅛in (29mm) thick by 1in (25mm) or so wide (see the plan of the top in Fig 3) – this width is determined by the need to mitre the lipping at the corners and to round them off. One of the virtues of MDF is that it can be machined easily and there should be no problem in grooving the edges to accept the tongues. The top veneer should, of course, extend over and almost up to the front edges of the lipping but a small gap of about ¹⁄₁₆in (2mm) needs to be worked into which the stringing should be glued; the front and end edges are veneered with a cross-grained veneer. Fig 1(A) is a squared-off drawing of the curves on the front edges of the frieze rail and the top, the latter being pocket-screwed in place.

Veneering and fans

These follow the methods described in Appendices 2 and 3. Those readers who prefer to buy in the fans rather than make them can obtain them from World of Wood (address in Suppliers' List on page 158).

Brasswork

Ring handles are available from many sources but H. E. Savill and Romany Tyzack (see Suppliers' List) have particularly good selections that are true to period.

Fig 3 Front and end elevations and plans. Also details of large drawer front and the fan inlay.

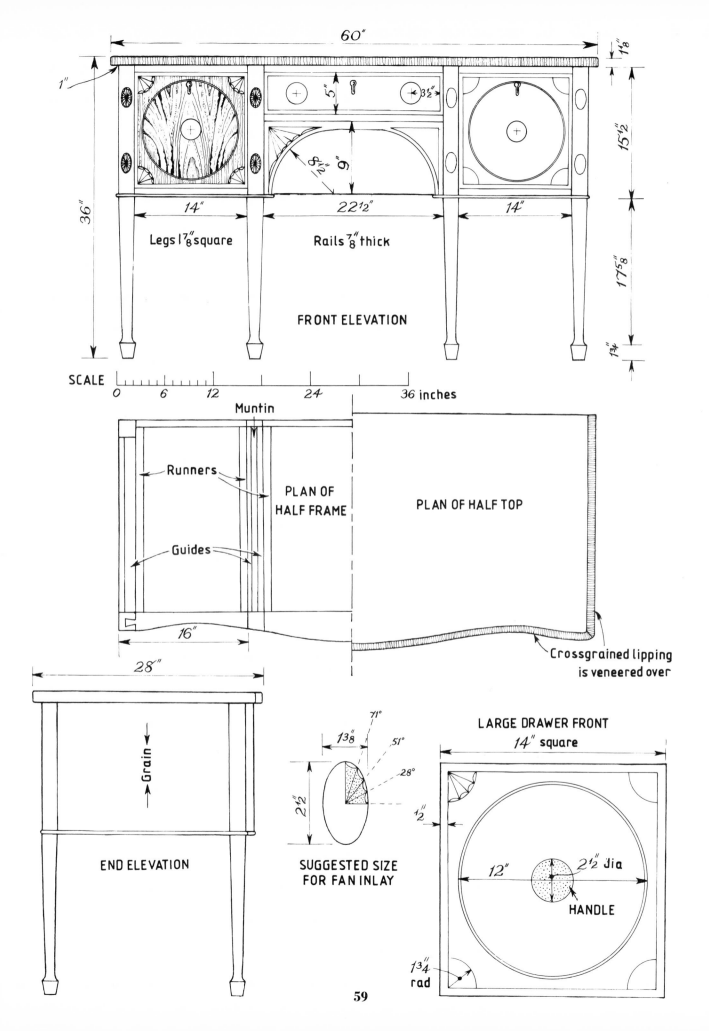

60"

1"

1⅛"

5"

3½"

15½"

8½"
9"

36"

14"
Legs 1⅞" square

22½"
Rails ⅞" thick

14"

17⅝"

1¾"

FRONT ELEVATION

SCALE

0   6   12   24   36 inches

Muntin

Runners

PLAN OF
HALF FRAME

PLAN OF HALF TOP

Guides

16"

Crossgrained lipping
is veneered over

28"

Grain

END ELEVATION

71°

13⅛"

51°

2½"

28°

SUGGESTED SIZE
FOR FAN INLAY

LARGE DRAWER FRONT
14" square

½"

12"

2½" dia

HANDLE

1¾"
rad

59

Finish

The authentic finish would be one made up as a shellac varnish, and details are given in Appendix 5.

Cutting List

	inches			*mm*		
	L	W	T	L	W	T
1 top (solid)	61	29	1⅛	1549	737	29
6 legs, each	38	2¼	1⅞	965	58	48
2 end panels, each	24	16	¾	610	407	19
2 intermediate panels, each	24	16	¾	610	407	19
2 outer back panels, each	16	16	⅜	407	407	10
1 central back panel	25	16	¾	635	407	19
1 frieze rail	61	4¼	⅞	1549	108	23
2 outer drawer rails, each	15½	2¾	⅞	394	70	23
1 central drawer rail	24	4¼	⅞	610	108	23
2 large drawer fronts, say 28 strips, each	16	2½	¾	407	64	19
2 large drawer backs, each	14½	14½	½	369	369	13
4 large drawer sides, each	24	14½	½	610	369	13
2 large drawer bottoms, each	25	14½	⅜	635	369	10
2 lippings for above, from 1 piece	16	3½	³⁄₁₆	407	89	5
1 central drawer front (solid, cut from 1 piece)	24	6	2½	610	152	64
1 central drawer back	24	6	⅜	610	152	10
2 central drawer sides, each	26	6	⅜	660	152	10
1 central drawer bottom	26	24	¼	660	610	6
2 lippings for above, from 1 piece	24	3½	³⁄₁₆	610	89	5
6 drawer guides, each	23½	1¾	¾	597	45	19
6 drawer runners, each	23½	1½	¾	597	38	19
1 length of drawer slip, cuts all	100	⅞	¾	2540	23	19
2 pieces to cut 4 spandrels	12	10	⅝	305	254	16

Generous working allowances have been made to lengths and widths; thicknesses are net.

TRIPOD TIP-TOP TABLE

One of those designs which has hardly altered since it first appeared in about 1750 and which is still popular today. Deservedly so, as it gracefully combines beauty and utility.

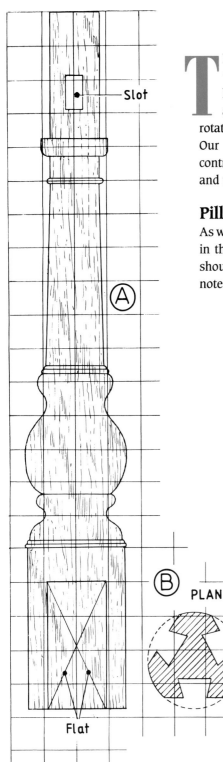

Fig 2 Elevation of table and plan of top; (A) details of birdcage; (B) section through top; (C) leg fixing details

This design is variously known as a 'tip-top', 'snap', 'claw' or 'pillar and claw' table, the term 'claw' referring to the style of leg. There are three variations, namely a table with a fixed top, a table with a revolving top, and one where the top can be rotated and also tilted so that the table may stand against a wall. Our design, in mahogany, is the last-named and contains a contrivance called a 'birdcage' that allows the top to both revolve and tilt. It is dated circa 1750. **Skill rating – 4.**

Pillar

As well as being illustrated in Fig 2, this is shown in greater detail in the 1in squared-off drawing in Fig 1. Although the turning should be straightforward enough, there are several points to note. At the top, the final 3½in (89mm) of the length needs to be

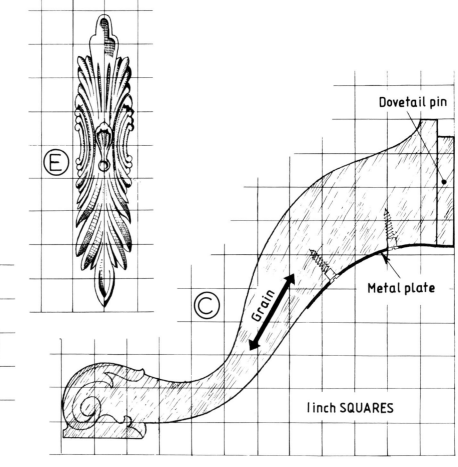

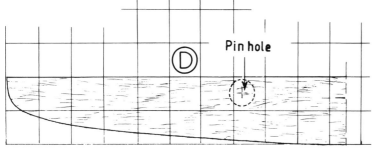

Fig 1 One-inch squared diagram showing (A) pillar; (B) plan of pillar base; (C) pattern of leg; (D) half elevation of a bearer; (E) detail of suggested carving on knee.

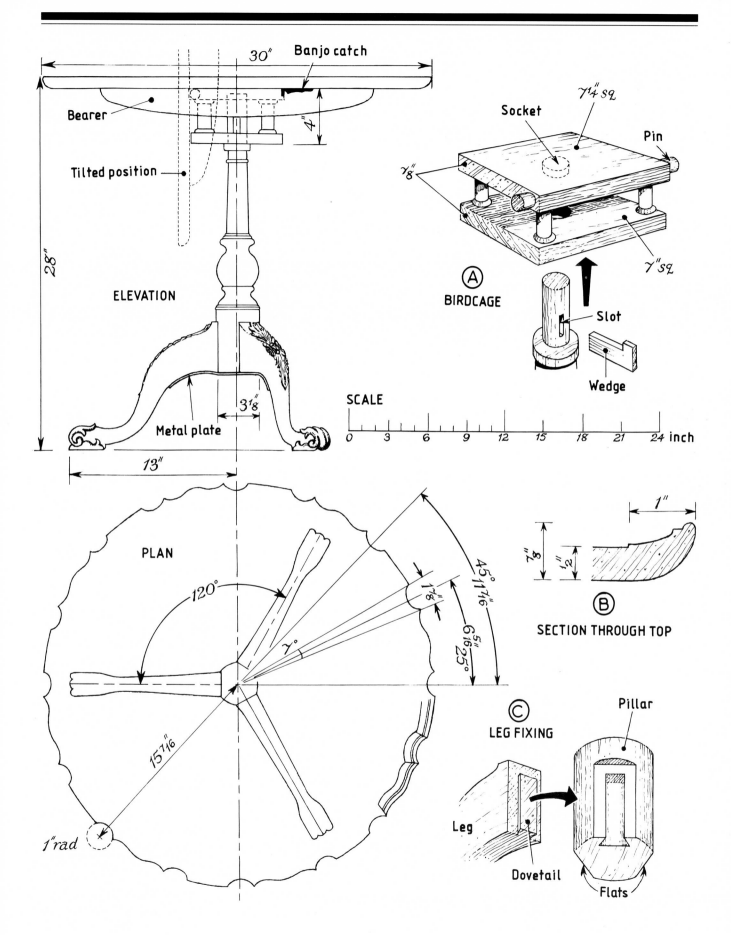

30"

Banjo catch

Bearer

Tilted position

28"

ELEVATION

4"

Socket

7¼" sq

Pin

⅞"

7" sq

Ⓐ BIRDCAGE

Slot

Wedge

3⅛"

Metal plate

13"

SCALE

0   3   6   9   12   15   18   21   24 inch

PLAN

120°

7°

1⅛"

45°
11 7/16"
6 5/16"
25°

15 7/16"

1" rad

1"

⅞"

½"

Ⓑ SECTION THROUGH TOP

Pillar

Ⓒ LEG FIXING

Leg

Dovetail

Flats

reduced to form a 1⅜in (35mm) diameter pin which at the same time creates a shoulder on the pillar on which the birdcage can revolve. A slot has to be cut right through the pin at the position shown in Fig 1, and a wedge inserted into this when the birdcage is finally assembled.

Also, accurate marking out of the flats to which the legs are jointed is required at the bottom of the pillar, and it is well worthwhile making a card template in the shape of a 3⅛in (80mm) disc; from the centre of this draw three radii at 120 degrees to each other. About ¼in (6mm) from the junction of each radius with the circumference draw a chord 1¾in (45mm) long; each of the three chords will then correspond with the 'flat' marked at Fig 1(A) and at Fig 2(C).

Legs

The shape of these can be plotted from the drawing at Fig 1(C). The three can be nested into one another to save timber, provided that the grain runs in the direction shown as this gives the greatest strength at the most vulnerable part. Although a bandsaw is the best tool for sawing them out, the job can be done equally efficiently with a bowsaw. A dovetail pin has to be worked on the lower end of each leg to join it to the pillar and this is shown at Fig 2(C), together with the matching sockets cut on the flats. Further details of the latter are given in the plan at Fig 1(B).

Cramping up this type of claw leg is always tricky and probably the best way is illustrated in Fig 3(A), where an open-ended box (made up from scrap) acts as an anchor for a sash or a deep-throated G-cramp.

The assembly has, of course, to be done before the legs are finally shaped and carved. Fig 1(E) shows the pattern of carving on the knees, known as coquillage. Unless you are an accomplished wood carver it would be better to leave the knees plain and concentrate on the whorled design on the toes as this should be simpler to do; the pattern is shown at Fig 1(C).

Fig 4 Stages in working the piecrust top. Also, (A) banjo catch; (B) metal plate for strengthening the leg fixings; (C) device for scribing around the top.

Fig 3 Suggested method for cramping up the legs is shown at (A); dimensions of bearer pin and birdcage pillar at (B) and (C) respectively.

Cramps indicated by heavy lines

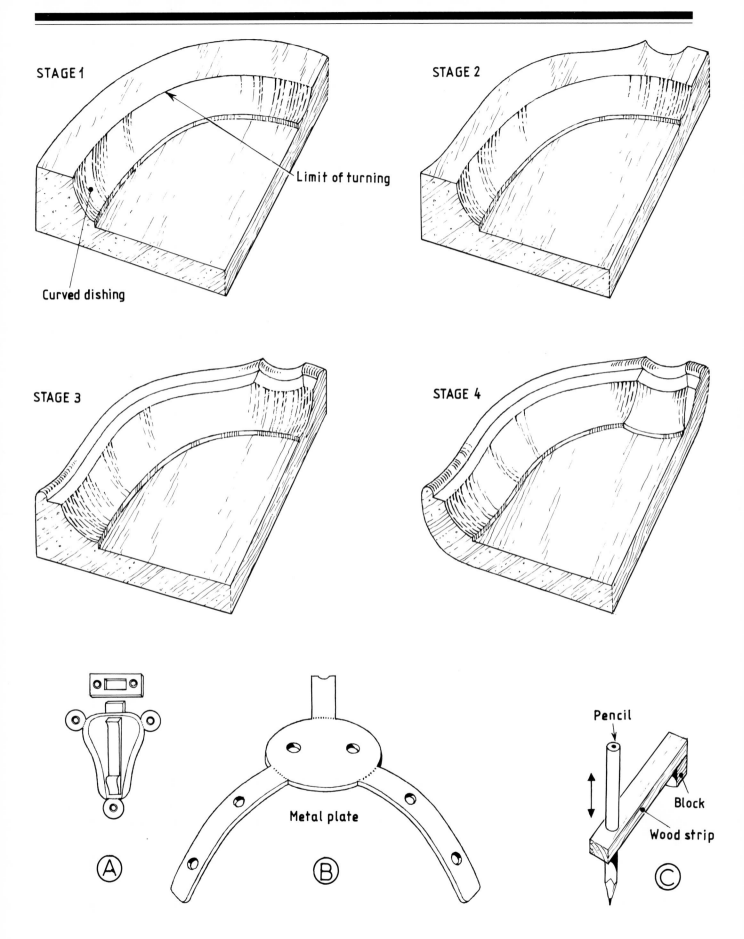

STAGE 1

Limit of turning

Curved dishing

STAGE 2

STAGE 3

STAGE 4

Metal plate

Pencil

Block

Wood strip

Ⓐ

Ⓑ

Ⓒ

Top

This is known as a 'piecrust' top, from the shape of the edge; and in genuine pieces it was always worked from the solid. Obviously the marking out must be precise, and by far the best way to ensure this is to draw the complete pattern on card or paper first and cut templates for the different shapes from it. The details are shown in the plan in Fig 2, and also in the section at Fig 2(B).

Unless you are fortunate enough to have a wide piece of mahogany from which the top can be cut in its entirety, it will have to be rub-jointed from two or possibly three pieces (this kind of joint is described in Appendix 1).

Traditionally, the dishing out to the limit shown in Fig 4, Stage 1, was done on the face plate of a lathe and this is still a practical way to do the job. A square block of ¾in (19mm) thick scrap wood can be screwed to the back of the top to take the centre; the screw holes can later be pelleted (see Appendix 1), or plugged and covered with baize.

Alternatively the job can be done with a power router by attaching a block of scrap wood to the centre of the top with double-sided adhesive tape and using it as a centre for the pin of the router's trammel rod. Using a flat-bottomed cutter, a channel can be routed out to correspond to the limit of turning marked in Fig 4, Stage 1; the block can then be removed and the remainder of the waste routed out freehand.

Carving the top

The first step is to achieve the result shown at Fig 4, Stage 2, by jigsawing round the outer shapes and this is where the card templates will prove invaluable. Stage 3 illustrates how the outermost members of the moulding are either carved or worked with a scratch-stock, or more likely by a combination of both.

Stage 4 is the most difficult and can only be carved. The scribing of the inner edge involves the pencil riding up and down the curved dishing as it follows the serpentine outer shapes. The device shown at Fig 4(C) should prove helpful and needs no explanation other than to point out that the pencil is a loose fit and is free to move up or down; the face of the scribing block which presses against the outer edge is slightly curved so that the shapes can be followed easily.

Alternative method of making the top

Undeniably a traditional piecrust top is a job for a wood carver rather than a cabinet maker. If you are not concerned with historical authenticity there is an easier way to make a reasonably accurate top by assembling the whole of the piecrust moulding from separate pieces which can be pinned and glued in place. Once the shapes have been sawn out, a power router can be used to work most of the moulding, although a certain amount will inevitably have to be finished by hand.

Birdcage and bearers

The sketch at Fig 2(A) depicts the birdcage, which consists of two blocks held apart by four small turned pillars, each of which has a small pin turned on both ends to provide a glued fixing into the blocks (see Fig 3(C) for dimensions).

A hole is cut centrally through the lower block to fit over the reduced end of the main pillar, which itself locates into a recessed socket cut to receive it at the centre of the underside of the upper block. This enables the whole sub-assembly to revolve while resting on the shoulder of the main pillar. Before the birdcage can be finally assembled, however, the upper block needs to be glued and screwed to the underside of the top at the exact centre and a wedge driven into the slot.

There are two identical bearers and a half-elevation of one of them is shown at Fig 1(D); the bearers are glued and screwed to the underside of the top so that they lie either side of the birdcage. Before this is done, two pins need to be turned up to the dimensions shown in Fig 3(B), and glued into one end of the birdcage block as shown at Fig 2(A) and in the elevation. These pins fit into the holes on the bearers so that not only can the top revolve but also tilt to a vertical position.

Metalwork

In order to prevent the top being accidentally tilted, a banjo catch (Fig 4(A)) is fitted as shown in the elevation in Fig 2. Although this is the authentic type of catch there are several other kinds of table catches, any of which will do the job equally well.

The metal plate, Fig 4(B), has to be custom-made from $1/16$in (2mm) mild steel and fits over the bottom end of the pillar, the arms being screwed to the undersides of the legs as shown at Fig 1(C).

Finishing

To be true to the period the table should be finished in shellac as described in Appendix 5.

Cutting List

	inches			mm		
	L	W	T	L	W	T
1 top	31	31	7/8	787	787	23
1 main pillar	22	3½	3⅛	559	89	80
3 legs, from one piece	33	10	1⅞	838	254	48
2 bearers, each	22	2¼	7/8	559	58	23
2 birdcage blocks, each	7¾	7½	7/8	197	190	23
4 birdcage pillars, each	4	1¾	1½	102	45	38
2 birdcage pins, each	1½	1	¾	38	25	19

Generous working allowances have been made to lengths and widths; thicknesses are net.

SHAKER ROCKING CHAIR

Grace, simplicity and fitness for purpose are the three attributes with which the Shakers endowed all their furniture, and this rocking chair displays them all. There were many similar designs produced at their several factories.

The 'Shakers' (properly called The United Society of Believers in Christ's Second Reappearing) were a religious society founded by Mother Ann Lee who emigrated to the USA from Manchester, England, in 1774. Their worship included a kind of shaking dance which gave them their nickname. They were renowned for their farming techniques and for the quality of their seeds and plants; in their work they followed the precept of their founder to 'Do all your work as though you had a thousand years to live, and as you would if you knew you must die tomorrow'.

Their furniture is renowned for having graceful elegance combined with functional simplicity. In 1863 they began to mass-produce chairs for the outside world at their community in Mount Lebanon, but the rocker illustrated is probably one from the workshop at Watervliet, New York, and was made between 1820 and 1866. **Skill rating – 2.**

General remarks

Shaker chairs were made from a variety of woods depending on local supplies but the favourite timber for the legs was maple; the hickory or ash they used is still the best wood for the ladderback slats as they both bend readily. Most of the dimensions are slightly stouter than on the original; for instance, the front and back legs are 1½in (38mm) in diameter instead of 1⅜in (35mm), and the back slats are ⅝in (16mm) instead of ⅜in (10mm).

Shaker chairs were made so that they could be hung on pegs in the walls of their meeting rooms and thus leave more floor space for their devotions; it is for this reason that the frame of this rocking chair is angled backwards.

Frame

The front legs and rungs can be turned on the lathe; note that in accordance with Shaker technique only the two front rungs are swelled, the remainder being straight cylinders with ¹⁄₁₆in (2mm) shoulders at each end which enter the legs and are glued in place.

It is unlikely that you will have a lathe bed long enough to accommodate the back legs as the largest size (for non-industrial machines) is normally 36in (914mm). Although the leg could be made in two sections glued together, for reasons of strength it would be better if shaped by hand. This is not as difficult as it may appear; once the square blank has been tapered, using a moulding box as described in Appendix 1, each edge is bevelled off by planing until you achieve an octagonal cross section, when the final rounding off can be done with a spokeshave and glasspaper.

There is one job to be done before you start the tapering, and that is to cut the mortises for the back slats in the positions shown in the side elevation, Fig 1 and at Fig 2(C). Each finial is turned separately with a pin at the lower end which is glued into a hole bored into the upper end of the back leg, and the shape is drawn as at Fig 1(A) on the squared-off drawing.

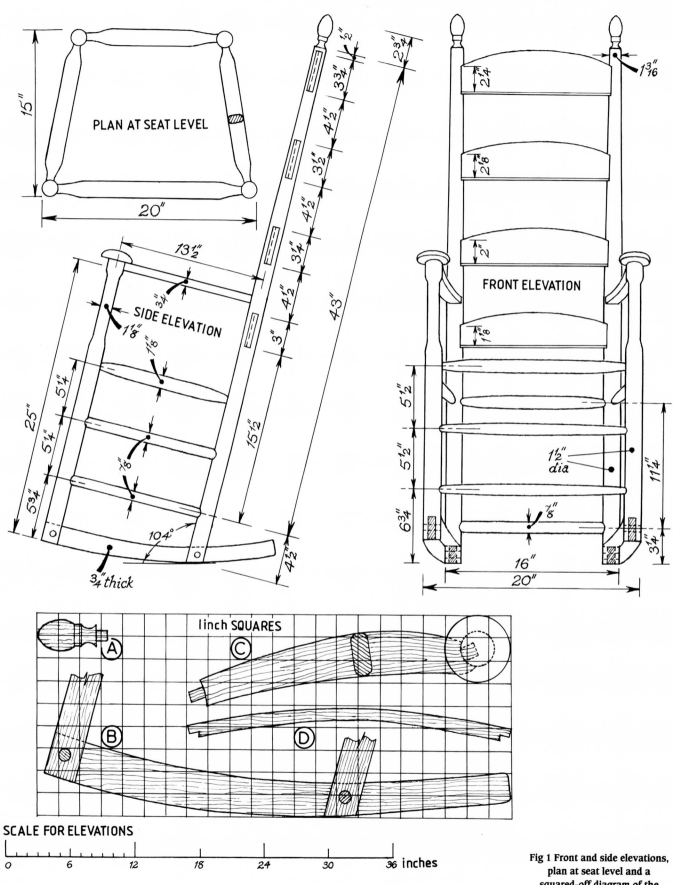

PLAN AT SEAT LEVEL

SIDE ELEVATION

FRONT ELEVATION

1 inch SQUARES

SCALE FOR ELEVATIONS

0   6   12   18   24   30   36 inches

Fig 1 Front and side elevations, plan at seat level and a squared-off diagram of the shaped parts.

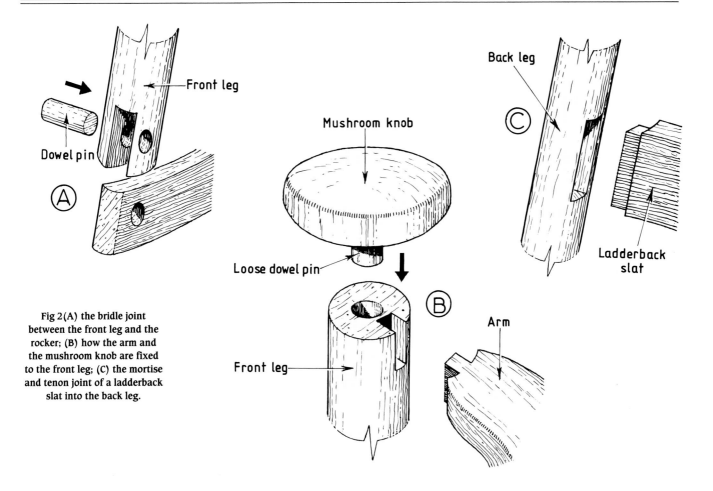

Fig 2 (A) the bridle joint between the front leg and the rocker; (B) how the arm and the mushroom knob are fixed to the front leg; (C) the mortise and tenon joint of a ladderback slat into the back leg.

Rockers and arms

The outline shapes of these are shown at (B) and (C) respectively in the squared-off drawing in Fig 1. The front legs are bridle-jointed over the rockers, the joints being glued and further secured with dowel pins. On many Shaker chairs screws were used instead of pins and the joints were not glued but left dry so that the parts could be dismantled if repairs were necessary.

The plan of an arm is drawn at (C) in the same diagram; there is a small tenon where it meets the back leg and this needs to be scribed to fit; similarly the tenon at the front end has to be worked at an angle and also scribed. The mushroom-shaped knob is glued in place by means of a loose dowel pin as shown at Fig 2 (B).

Back slats

These are slightly curved, about ⅞in (22mm) – as at Fig 1 (D) – and need to be steamed for an hour before being bent. Cut them oversize to about 18in (458mm) and stand them on a wooden block inside a metal container so that they stand clear of the water; the container should have some kind of lid, which you can make from scrap wood, and a rag-plugged 'safety-valve' as shown on page 29. Only a couple of inches of water are needed, which can be replenished from time to time with boiling water from a kettle. The container will need to be supported on some bricks over the heat source, which can be a camping gas stove.

71

Test the slats every twenty minutes or so and when they are flexible enough transfer them to a shaping matrix. This is simply a piece of ¾in (19mm) plywood or chipboard on which the outline of the curved shape is followed by some nails hammered partway in so that they protrude by about 1in (25mm), and spaced about 3in (76mm) apart. Leave the slats to dry out and when they have assumed the correct curve you can work the tenons on the ends as shown in Fig 2(C).

Seat

As you can see from the seat plan in Fig 1, the seat rails are reduced at their ends and also have their edges well rounded, this being the shape required if you decide to have the seats finished with rushing.

The Shakers, however, used not only rush as a seating material but also splint or cane or a worsted tape. The chair illustrated has its seat made of interwoven splints, which are thin strips of hickory about ⅜in (10mm) wide by ¹⁄₁₆in (2mm) thick, varnished over. The taped seats were also interwoven with 1in (25mm) wide 'listing' or worsted tape, and both methods utilize the kind of seat rails described above.

Neither of these materials is obtainable in the UK, but cane could be used as an alternative. Caned seats require the normal style of seat rails but they need to be laid flat and not upright. Lengths of rattan cane can be bought in various widths; all you need to do is to damp it lightly and tack or staple it in place, trim off the excess, and cover the tack heads with a strip of cane fixed with the smallest size of veneer pin. Alternatively you could have the work carried out professionally. Varnishing afterwards will prevent the seat becoming soiled with use.

Finish

The earliest chairs were painted with milk-paint (usually red) or stained with a diluted version of it so that the grain showed through. Later designs such as the one we are discussing were usually finished with linseed oil or a clear shellac varnish.

Cutting List

	inches L	W	T	mm L	W	T
2 back legs, each	49	2	1½	1244	51	38
2 front legs, each	26½	2	1½	673	51	38
2 rockers, each	23	4	¾	584	102	19
1 top slat	16	4¼	⅝	407	108	16
1 upper middle slat	16	4	⅝	407	102	16
1 lower middle slat	16	3¾	⅝	407	95	16
1 bottom slat	16	3½	⅝	407	89	16
2 arms, each	15	3½	¾	381	89	19
2 front underframe rails, each	20½	1⅛	⅞	521	29	22
4 side underframe rails, each	15	1⅛	⅞	381	29	22
1 back underframe rail	16	1⅛	⅞	407	29	22
1 front seat rail	20½	1¾	1⅛	521	45	29
1 back seat rail	16	1¾	1⅛	407	45	29
2 side seat rails, each	15	1¾	1⅛	381	45	29
2 mushroom knob blanks, each	4	3½	¾	102	89	19
2 finials, each	3¼	1½	1¼	83	38	32

Generous working allowances have been made to lengths and widths; thicknesses are net.

OAK DRESSER

Like the Windsor chair, this is a perennially popular design that has hardly changed over the past 200 years — a supreme example of utility combined with an attractive appearance and a piece of furniture which can be found in thousands of homes today.

This is a dresser of about 1775 which is almost certainly Welsh although it is notoriously difficult to determine both the origin and the date of a design like this; it could have been made at any time during the period 1720 to 1820. Dressers were also made in Lancashire and Yorkshire and these often have small cupboards (and sometimes clocks) in the plate rack section; those made in the West Country tend to be one-piece designs in which the upper and lower parts are integrally joined. **Skill rating – 3.**

General remarks

The overall height is 77in (1955mm) and the dresser will therefore fit comfortably into a modern room. The plate rack section simply sits on top of the bottom cupboard part and this is quite usual, although the two were sometimes joined together by wooden or metal fastenings at the back. It appears that an attempt has been made to make the piece illustrated look more fashionable by fixing bracket feet to the front posts and covering their upper edges with a moulding. These feet could well be dispensed with.

Ordinary softwood could be used instead of oak as it is readily obtainable and is better from the point of view of timber conservation. If you decide to do this, resist the temptation to use tongued and grooved boards either in the doors or the back of the upper section as it is not historically accurate. It is most unlikely that you will be able to buy oak thin enough for the various panels and drawer bottoms, and the best expedient is to use oak-veneered plywood.

Top of cupboard section

This could not be more straightforward as it is simply one piece of oak, or two pieces rub-jointed together (see Appendix 1) if you cannot get one board of sufficient width; the edges of the front and ends are moulded while the back edge is left square. The top can be pocket-screwed (Appendix 1) to the frame rails.

Carcase framing

This is illustrated in Fig 1, and the construction is complicated by the fact that the muntins (H) for the upper drawers are not vertically in line with the lower ones; this results in the need for the extra drawer runners (M) as shown. Each drawer runner has a drawer guide glued and screwed to it but the guides have been omitted from the illustration for clarity. The drawer framing follows the style described in Appendix 1.

Another anomaly is that the lower end rails (B) do not line up with the back and front rails (C) and (D); this necessitates the provision of two fillets (P), one at the front and the other at the back, to which the bottom boards are screwed. In each cupboard a middle shelf (not shown) rests on and is screwed to a fillet (R) on the end rail (G), and to another screwed to the opposite drawer rail. Two panels are grooved into each end; and an intermediate

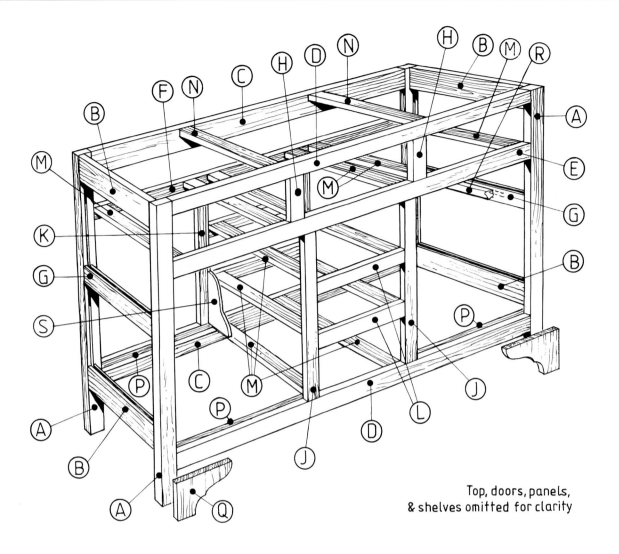

Top, doors, panels,
& shelves omitted for clarity

panel (S) is pinned to the drawer rails on each side of the central drawers.

Fig 1 Perspective drawing of carcase framing.

Mortise and tenon joints should be employed throughout if you wish to be historically correct as dowelled joints were not used until the 1850s.

Doors

As you can see from the photograph and Figs 2 and 3 (B), the upper rail on each door is notched out into a stepped shape, and the panel is likewise notched to follow it, leaving a ½in (13mm) wide channel between them all round. Clearly, grooving the panel into the door frame in the usual manner would present no special problems until the notched steps have to be dealt with, as it would be tricky to work the groove on them. An easier way is shown in Fig 3 (B) where, instead of being grooved in, the panel lies in a rebate worked on the inside edges of the door frame, and a covering beading is pinned (but not glued) around the edges to give a neat finish.

Some of the old-time craftsmen made provision for the possibility of the panel shrinking by driving the pins into narrow slits cut

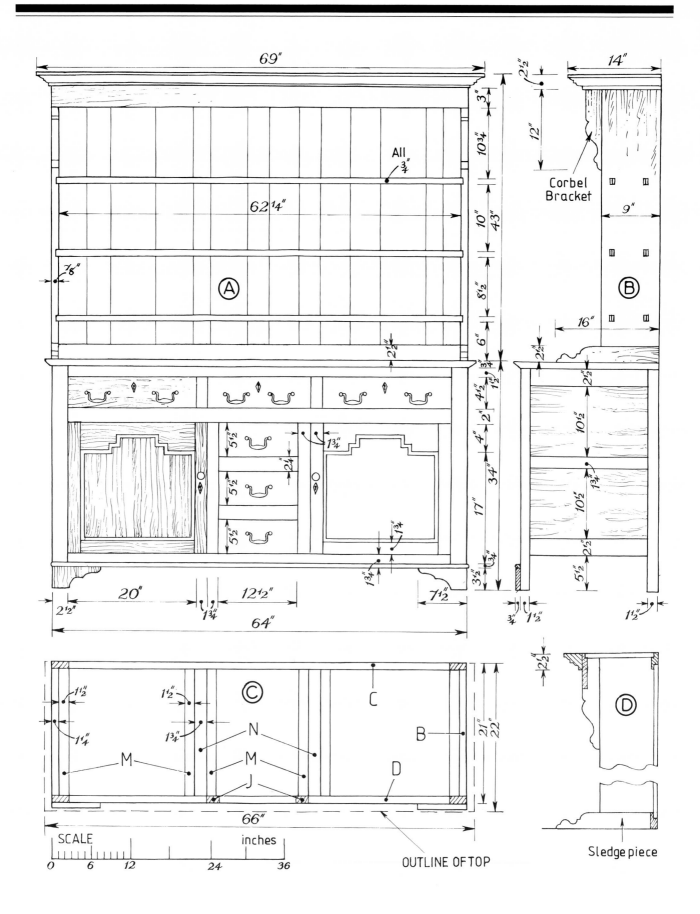

SCALE   inches

0   6   12   24   36

OUTLINE OF TOP

Corbel Bracket

Sledge piece

Fig 3(A) squared-off drawings
of corbel bracket and sledge
piece; (B) detail of notches
on door panel and stile;
(C) sketch of wedged tenons;
(D) detail of drawer.

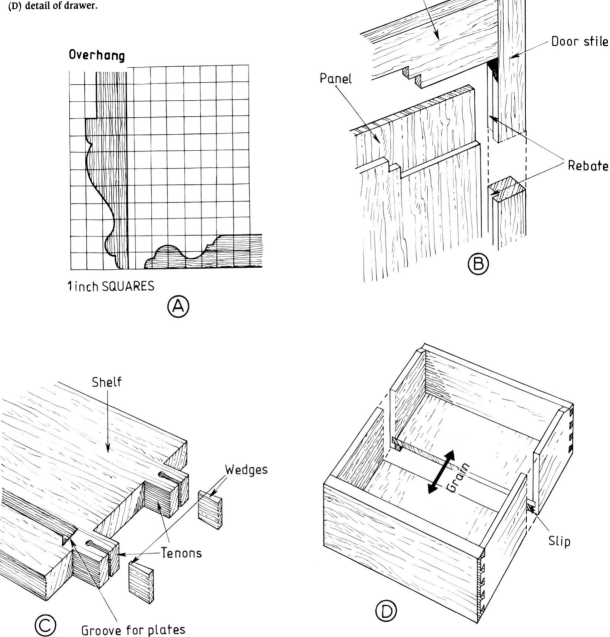

Overhang

1 inch SQUARES

Ⓐ

Upper rail

Door stile

Panel

Rebate

Ⓑ

Shelf

Wedges

Tenons

Ⓒ

Groove for plates

Grain

Slip

Ⓓ

in the edges of the panel – thus although the beading held the panel
down into the rebate it was free to shrink across the grain.

Drawers

These are shown in Fig 3 (D) and are of the orthodox pattern. Note
that the grain of the drawer bottom runs from front to back, and
this means that drawer slips should be pinned and glued to the
drawer sides to accommodate any shrinkage across the width, and
at the same time provide extra support.

Fig 2(A) front elevation;
(B) end elevation; (C) plan;
(D) section of end.

Plate rack section

This is a straightforward piece of work, and the only special feature is that the shelves are recessed into ¼in (6mm) deep trenches cut in the ends; two tenons are cut on the end of each shelf as shown in Fig 3(C) and then wedged. The slit for each wedge should not extend to the root of the tenon but only about three-quarters of the distance; a small hole is drilled at the end of the slit to prevent it from splitting farther. It helps if you ease out the mortises on the plate rack ends so that they become slightly wedge-shaped, thus allowing the tenons to expand without being distorted when the wedges are driven in. Make the wedges slightly over-long so that the excess can be trimmed off after fixing.

A groove can be cut towards the front of each shelf as shown at Fig 3(C) to prevent the plates from slipping forward; the alternative (and better) method is to fix on a small beading with panel pins to serve the same purpose – this can then always be unpinned and refixed when necessary.

The backs of most dressers of this period are similar in that they consist of boards of random width simply butted alongside each other (Fig 2(A)) and nailed or screwed into rebates on the back edges of the tops, ends and bottom rails; the boards were very rarely tongued and grooved. Fig 2(D) shows the method in section.

Brasswork

This comprises lifting bail handles, plain circular knobs, and diamond-shaped escutcheons, all of which are widely obtainable.

Finish

An oak piece like this should be stained so that all parts match in colour, following this with a couple of coats of clear shellac to prevent dust being rubbed into the grain, and then wax polished (see Appendix 5).

Cutting List

	inches			mm		
	L	W	T	L	W	T
Plate rack section						
1 top	66	12	½	1676	305	13
1 fascia front rail	65	6	¾	1651	152	19
2 ends, each	41	9½	⅞	1041	241	23
1 top back rail	65	3	⅞	1651	76	23
1 front moulding	71	3	2½	1803	76	64
2 end mouldings, each	15	3	2½	381	76	64
2 corbel brackets, each	13	3	⅞	330	76	23
1 bottom back rail	65	3	⅞	1651	76	23
2 shaped sledge pieces, each	17	3	⅞	432	76	23
3 shelves, each	63	9¼	¾	1600	235	19
Backboards, to fill a space	64	41	½	1625	1041	13

Cupboard section						
1 top	68	23	¾	1727	584	19
4 corner posts (A), each	34	3	1½	864	76	38
4 end rails (B), each	20	3	¾	508	76	19
2 back rails (C), each	62	3	¾	1575	76	19
2 front rails (D), each	62	3	¾	1575	76	19
1 middle front rail (E)	62	2½	¾	1575	64	19
1 middle back rail (F)	62	2½	¾	1575	64	19
2 middle end rails (G), each	21	2¼	¾	533	57	19
2 upper muntins (H), each	6	2¼	¾	152	57	19
2 lower muntins (J), each	21	2¼	¾	533	57	19
2 vertical back muntins (K), each	21	2¼	¾	533	57	19

	in	in	in	mm	mm	mm
2 drawer rails (L), each	14	2¾	¾	356	70	19
12 drawer runners (M), each	21	1¾	¾	533	45	19
2 kickers (N), each	21	2¼	¾	533	57	19
4 fillets (P), each	22	1¾	¾	559	45	19
2 bracket feet (Q), optional, each	8	4	¾	204	102	19
2 shelf fillets (R), each	21	1¾	¾	533	45	19
2 panels (S), each	21	21	½	533	533	13
4 end panels, each	19½	11	½	495	280	13
12 drawer guides, each	21	1¼	¾	533	32	19

Doors

	in	in	in	mm	mm	mm
4 stiles, each	22	2¼	¾	559	57	19
2 upper rails, each	23	4½	¾	584	115	19
2 lower rails, each	23	2¼	¾	584	58	19
2 panels, each	17½	19	½	445	483	13

Upper drawers

	in	in	in	mm	mm	mm
2 fronts, outer drawers, each	21	5	¾	533	127	19
1 front, central drawer	17	5	¾	432	127	19
6 sides, each	20	5	½	508	127	13
2 backs, outer drawers, each	21	5	½	533	127	13
1 back, central drawer	17	5	½	432	127	13
2 bottoms, outer drawers, each	20	21	¼	508	533	6
1 bottom, central drawer	17	21	¼	432	533	6

Small drawers

	in	in	in	mm	mm	mm
3 fronts, each	13½	6	¾	343	153	19
6 sides, each	20	6	½	508	153	13
3 backs, each	13½	6	½	343	153	13
3 bottoms, each	13½	20	¼	343	508	6

Moulding (optional)

	in	in	in	mm	mm	mm
1 front length	66	1	¾	305	25	19

Generous working allowances have been made to lengths and widths; thicknesses are net.

WRITING BOX

*Although modern technology is
rapidly supplanting letter writing,
there are still many people who would
be delighted to receive this as a gift and
a reminder of the days of more
gracious living.*

Also called a 'writing slope'. This piece is exceptional in that it has a full provenance which is as follows: 'Regency (circa 1810) brass-bound fine quality writing box No 3705, bearing a trade label with the Royal Arms and made by Nicholas Middleton, 162 Strand Lane, London, Stationer to the King and the Prince of Wales.' It is made in mahogany and displays the highest workmanship; it is also well fitted out and the amount of brass strapping indicates that it probably belonged to a high-ranking military officer. **Skill rating** – 2.

Construction

It is advisable to cut the parts for the case from one plank so that the grain will follow round: the pieces that yield parts (A) and (B) in Fig 2 should be cramped together before sawing so that the 10 degree angle of slope is identical on both, and the top edges of (C), (D), (E) and (F) also need to be bevelled at precisely the same angle. Note that the drawer aperture in part (B) has to be sawn out, and you can use a jigsaw for this; obviously you will require another separate piece from the plank you have used for the drawer front.

To conform to the construction of the period the corners should be secret-mitre-dovetailed together (see Appendix 1); alternatively you could employ a tongued mitred joint as used for the cheese coaster on page 29 but you would have to house the tongue in a slot so that it does not show at the ends. These corners are the kind that can be very effectively made with a biscuit jointer, if you have one.

Note that the ends (E) and (F) are notched out along their top edges to accept the writing slopes (G) and (H) which are themselves hinged together and also notched at the inner corners. These slopes were always solid wood in the antique designs and consequently they often split, but to avoid this you could use 16mm plywood with mahogany veneers on both sides; the inside faces are lined with baize which is glued on in just the same way as leather (see Appendix 6). You would, of course, have to glue and pin on lippings round the edges of the plywood to hide the laminations.

Parts (L) and (M) form the top and bottom of the box and should be cut from the same plank as parts (A) and (B); they are grooved and rebated in as shown in the section in Fig 1 and also in Fig 2.

There is an inner floor (K), Fig 2, which covers the drawer and extends under the pen tray to be grooved into part (C); it is shown in the section in Fig 1 and again in Fig 2, as is the vertical division (J). The slopes are supported on the fillets (N) which are glued and screwed to the sides (see Fig 2).

The drawer in the photograph is beautifully lined with red Morocco leather and has slots to hold (presumably) envelopes and writing paper. You could leave the drawer empty or sub-divide it as you wish. It is made in the conventional manner as described

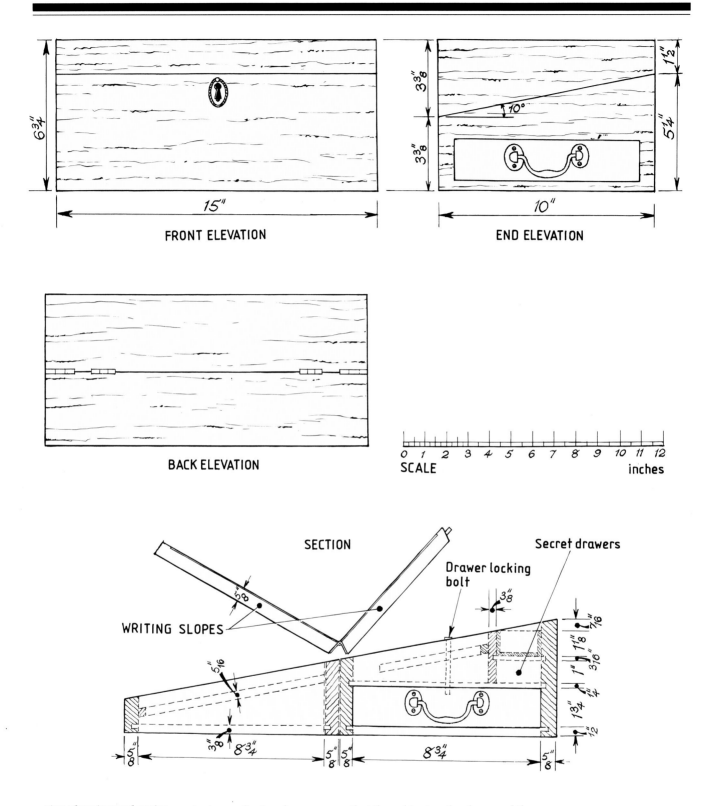

FRONT ELEVATION

END ELEVATION

BACK ELEVATION

SCALE

inches

SECTION

WRITING SLOPES

Secret drawers

Drawer locking bolt

Fig 1 Elevations and section.

in Appendix 1 and you can see that the cabinet maker has used the delicate needle-pin dovetails of the period.

Thin $^3/_{16}$in (5mm) stuff is used for the pen tray, the divisions being grooved and glued in (this will be discussed further below). Again, how you sub-divide the tray is up to you, largely depending on whether you wish to incorporate an inkwell; if so the size of the divisions will be governed by its dimensions.

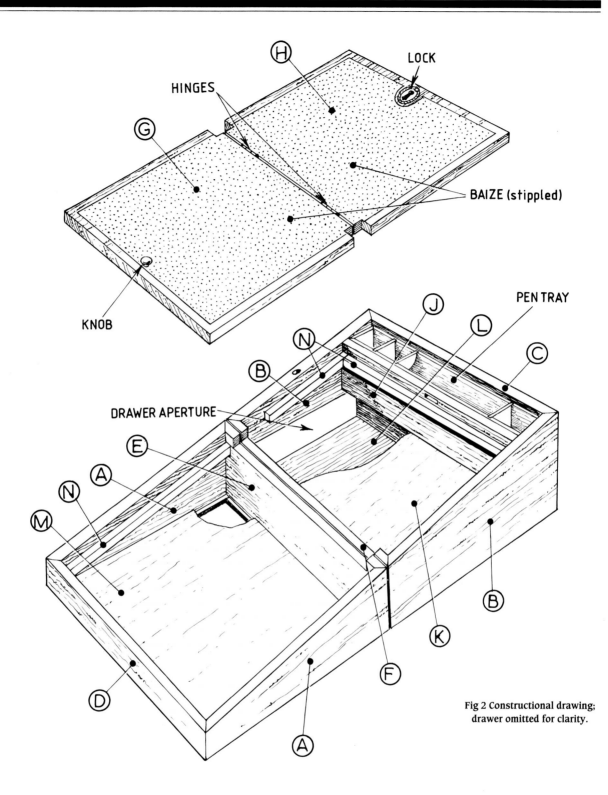

HINGES

LOCK

G

H

BAIZE (stippled)

KNOB

PEN TRAY

N

J

L

C

B

DRAWER APERTURE

E

N

A

M

F

K

B

D

A

Fig 2 Constructional drawing;
drawer omitted for clarity.

Secret drawers

The space for such drawers is shown in the section in Fig 1 and is underneath the pen tray; how you arrange them to work has to be your secret but one suggestion is that the divisions in the pen tray could be made to lift out to reveal them. Alternatively, the main drawer could be reduced in depth so that the secret drawers could be located at the back and held in place by small catches.

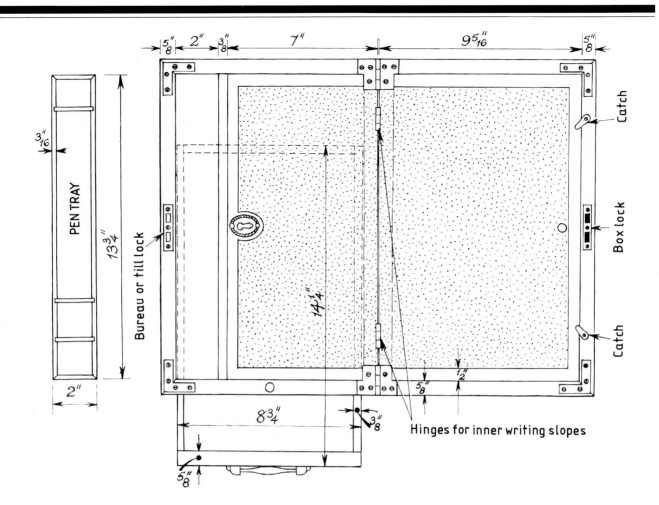

Fig 3 Plan to same scale as Fig 1.

Brasswork

Most writing boxes for domestic use did not carry the strapping shown in the photograph but if you would like to have some brass to complement the mahogany, some 'military chest' patterns are shown in Fig 4.

However, there are still two items of brassware that are non-standard, namely the right-angled corner straps and the shaped hinges that join parts (E) and (F), and you will have to prepare these yourself. The corner straps can be sawn from $\frac{1}{16}$in (16 SWG) brass sheet, which could also be used for any other brasswork you want to incorporate; this can be obtained from several firms quoted in the Suppliers' List on page 158. Special blades for sawing metal are readily available; a useful tip is to sandwich the brass sheet between two pieces of hardboard with the pattern marked on the top piece and saw and drill through the whole thing. Romany Tyzack (see Suppliers' List) can supply plain brass backflaps (No HG50717) which you can saw to the L-shape shown in Fig 3 and drill and countersink the requisite screw holes.

You will also need two locks – a box lock for the main case, and a bureau or till lock for the inner writing slope. The drawer is held closed by an ingenious device consisting of a brass rod fitted with a small cap; this drops through a hole bored right through side (A) in the position shown in Figs 1 and 3 and into a hole drilled in the

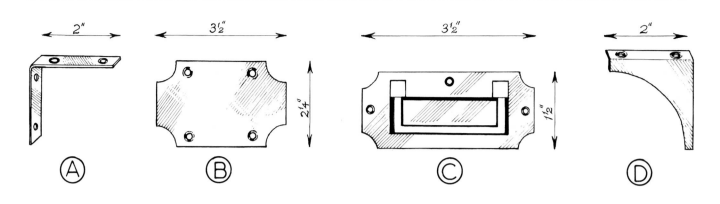

Fig 4 Some examples of suitable 'military chest' brasswork: (A) right-angled strap; (B) nameplate; (C) flush handle; (D) corner.

upper edge of the drawer front – this ensures that the drawer cannot be withdrawn until the box is unlocked and opened. Note that you will have to make a shallow depression on the opposite edge to receive the bolt head.

As well as the brass knob and catches shown in Fig 3 there is a long brass hinged strip on the side of the larger box. This acted as an adjustable support stay for the hinged writing slope which could then be used as a book rest.* Such fittings have to be specially made these days but you could use the alternative device of a wooden rod fitted with a brass cap at each end which could be inserted into holes bored in the appropriate positions.

If you wish to 'antique' the brass to give it a more traditional appearance, Liberon Waxes (see Suppliers' List) can supply a cleaning primer which is followed by a special solution that colours the brass to the required degree.

Finish

The shellac varnish described in Appendix 5 would be most suitable.

Cutting List

	inches			mm		
	L	W	T	L	W	T
2 parts (A) and 2 parts (B) from one piece	22	7½	⅝	559	191	16
1 end (c)	16	6	⅝	406	152	16
1 end (D)	16	2	⅝	406	51	16
1 inner end (E)	16	4	⅝	406	102	16
1 inner end (F)	16	4½	⅝	406	115	16
1 writing slope (G)	14½	10	⅝	368	254	16
1 writing slope (H)	14½	7½	⅝	368	191	16
1 division (J)	14½	3	⅜	368	76	10
1 floor (K)	14½	9½	¼	368	241	6
1 bottom (L)	15	10	½	381	254	13
1 top (M)	15½	10	½	394	254	13
1 fillet (N), cuts all	56	¾	½	1422	16	13

Pen tray

	inches			mm		
2 long sides, each	14½	1½	3/16	368	38	5
2 ends, each	2½	1½	3/16	64	38	5
1 bottom	14	2¼	3/16	356	58	5
Divisions, number to choice, each	2½	1½	⅛	64	38	3

Drawer

	inches			mm		
1 front	9½	2¼	⅝	241	58	16
2 sides, each	14½	2¼	⅜	368	58	10
1 back	9½	2¼	⅜	241	58	10
1 bottom	14¾	9¼	¼	375	235	6

Generous working allowances have been made to lengths and widths; thicknesses are net.

---

* I am most grateful to Mr John Biggs of J. Collins & Son for this information.

BUN-FOOT BUREAU

There is no need to emphasize how convenient it is to have a bureau in which to keep important papers and documents, and our design combines this facility with the handsome appearance of an original piece from the end of the 17th century.

This is a design belonging to the period around the end of the 17th century when bureaux of the style we know today were developing from desks which were mounted on underframes, and there are several characteristics which enable us to date them accurately.

One is that the upper section with the fall front is completely separate and can be lifted off – indeed, in some instances handles were fixed at the ends to make the job easier – the purpose being that in the days before banks and safety deposits the owners could take their valuables with them when travelling.

Another is that turned bun feet were replaced by the more familiar corner bracket feet from about 1710 onwards: also the new fashion of veneering, which had been introduced from Holland after the Restoration in 1660, was being over-indulged by English cabinet makers to the extent that all exteriors had to be veneered vertically regardless of practical considerations. This led to such risky practices as veneering over dovetailed joints and on to mouldings, and it is rare to find an example without split or buckled veneers, or both. **Skill rating – 4.**

General remarks

Although some bureaux were made in solid oak, most were in Baltic red pine (not the yellow pine which is frequently quoted as this refers to the wood from Canada) and veneered with the sawcut veneer of the time which was much thicker than the modern kind – $1/24$in or $1/16$in (1.0 or 1.6mm) compared with today's $1/32$in or 0.8mm.

Our design retains the feature of the two separate sections, and a moulding is planted around the top edge of the lower unit and projects enough to ensure the upper unit can be located easily.

The use of solid panels as drawer divisions instead of drawer rails, runners and the like, has been retained as it is typical of the period.

Carcases

The fact that both sections are built up from solid panels allows you a choice of materials and methods. The most obvious wood to use is pine, but most modern varieties are liable to carry too many knots and be resinous, and these defects can play havoc with veneers. Other suitable timbers are oak, gaboon, obeche, or Parana pine, all of which will need counter-veneering with oak veneer. Those who do not object to man-made boards will find MDF (medium density fibre board) an excellent choice, but again, this will need veneering with walnut as the exterior veneer and oak as the inner, counter-veneer. (For details of veneering techniques, see Appendix 2.)

If you do use natural timber, you will almost certainly need to rub-joint the component strips together to make up the requisite width; this process is described in Appendix 1.

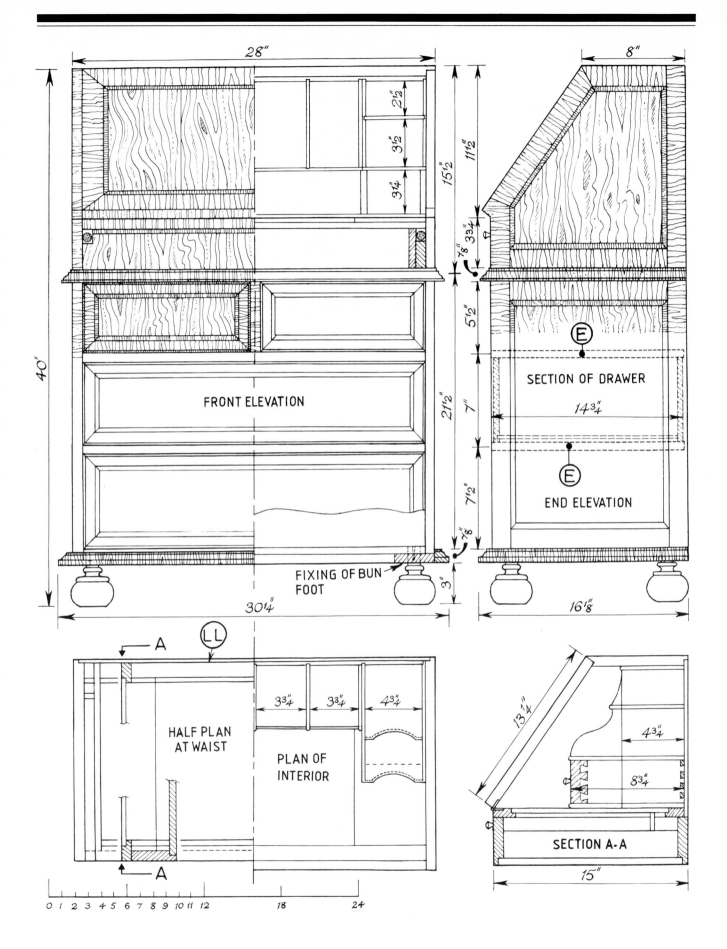

28"

2½"

3½"

3¾"

15½"

11½"

8"

FRONT ELEVATION

SECTION OF DRAWER

14¾"

END ELEVATION

40"

5½"

7"

21½"

7½"

⅞"

3¾"

⅞"

FIXING OF BUN FOOT

3"

30¼"

16'8"

A

LL

HALF PLAN AT WAIST

3¾"   3¾"   4¾"

PLAN OF INTERIOR

13¾"

4¾"

8¾"

SECTION A-A

15"

A

0 1 2 3 4 5 6 7 8 9 10 11 12   18   24

Fig 1 Elevations, plans, and sections.

Fig 2 shows both carcases lap-dovetailed together which is probably the most historically accurate method, although through dovetailed joints were also employed. Both kinds can readily be machined with a power router and a dovetailing accessory, or cut by hand; the more elegant secret mitred dovetail (described in Appendix 1) could be used but it can only be hand-cut. Perfectly good dovetailed joints can be made in MDF boards, and if you are more concerned with speed than authenticity there is no reason why you should not use biscuit joints.

The drawer division panels (E) are housed into the ends (A), and the vertical division (F) is similarly housed into (E) and (G). The whole carcase can then be fixed to the frame which comprises rails (M), (N) and the square blocks (O). These blocks have holes bored centrally to accept the pins turned on the bun feet; each pin is wedged in place as shown in the squared-off drawing in Fig 2.

Bureau section

As is customary with bureaux of the period, this section contains a well in addition to the usual pigeonhole fitting, and this tends to complicate the construction as the panel covering the well has to be capable of being lifted out as shown, or alternatively made to slide.

Fig 2 shows how this is achieved by means of the frame consisting of parts (Q) and (R); at each end there is a small assembly (parts (S) and (T)) enclosing a loper (U) which can be slid outwards to support the fall when it is open.

The pigeonhole section is shown in the upper small drawing, Fig 2(A), and is best made as a separate unit, although it must be said that in many examples the top and bottom panels were housed directly into the ends. The shelves and divisions are half-housed into each other, and a small quadrant moulding is planted around the lower edge. Dimensions are given in Fig 1. You can, of course, adapt the arrangement of the pigeonholes to suit yourself, bearing in mind that the stepped pattern was most popular until about 1725, and from then it was gradually superseded by the straight, vertical front.

Small knobs or leather tabs can be fixed to the panel covering the well so that it can be lifted out. Fig 2(A) shows an optional lining, although you may wish to omit this as it is not historically accurate.

Fall

Details of this are illustrated in Fig 1; it must be emphasized that unless constructed properly it will continually give trouble not only because of shrinkage but also due to the strain of being continually opened and closed.

Fig 3(A) illustrates how the fall should be made if it consists of rub-jointed solid walnut strips; these should be arranged with the heart sides opposed (see Appendix 1). A clamp can be fixed at right angles on each end either by means of wide mortise and tenon joints or by gluing in a cross-grained tongue. Either method should result in a stable construction.

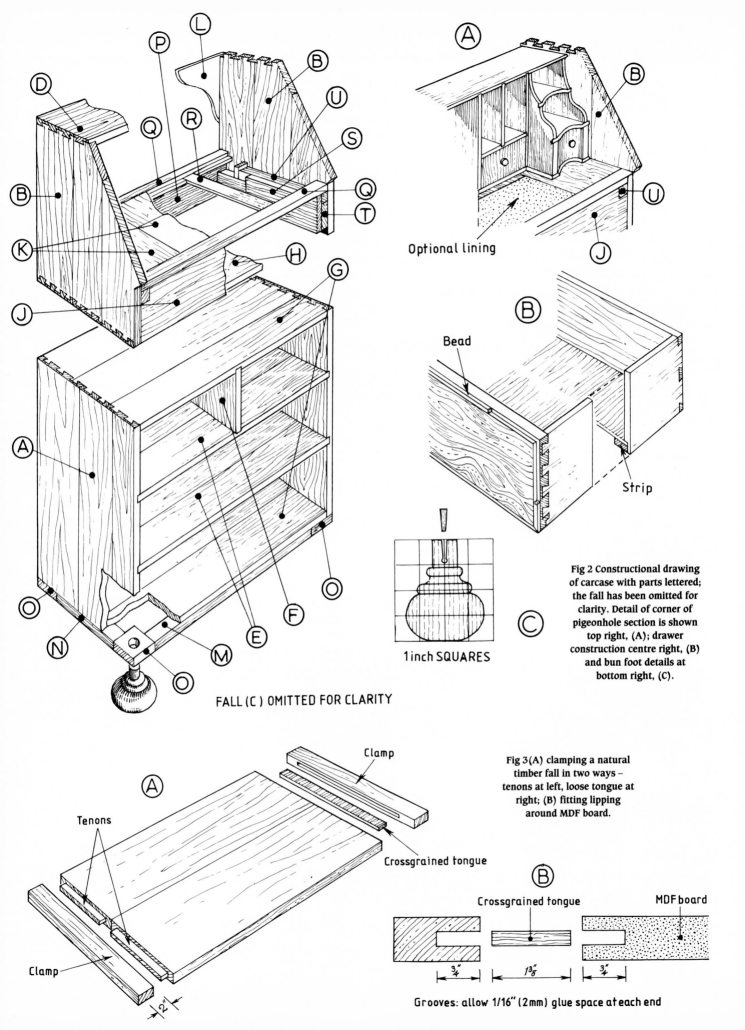

D

L

P

B

Q

R

U

B

S

U

K

Q

T

J

H

G

A

O

J

N

F

O

E

M

O

FALL (C) OMITTED FOR CLARITY

A

B

U

J

Optional lining

B

Bead

Strip

C

1 inch SQUARES

Fig 2 Constructional drawing of carcase with parts lettered; the fall has been omitted for clarity. Detail of corner of pigeonhole section is shown top right, (A); drawer construction centre right, (B) and bun foot details at bottom right, (C).

Clamp

Fig 3 (A) clamping a natural timber fall in two ways – tenons at left, loose tongue at right; (B) fitting lipping around MDF board.

A

Tenons

Crossgrained tongue

Clamp

2"

B

Crossgrained tongue

MDF board

$\frac{3}{4}$"

$1\frac{3}{8}$"

$\frac{3}{4}$"

Grooves: allow 1/16" (2mm) glue space at each end

Using a man-made board will of course avoid shrinkage problems but it will necessitate a wide lipping of solid walnut being tongued on all round and mitred at the corners (see Fig 3(B)), the walnut veneers being glued on afterwards.

Drawers

A corner detail of one of these is shown in the lower small drawing (B) in Fig 2; they are all constructed similarly. Generally they were made of oak or pine throughout, with the fronts lap-dovetailed to the sides; the walnut veneer facings were glued to the fronts with a thin bead planted all round – the size of the bead was determined by the thickness of the veneer.

The grain of the drawer bottom runs from front to back as was usual during the period, and it is checked into the lower edges of the sides and the front with a strip nailed on at each side which acts as a bearer.

Veneering

This is described in general terms in Appendix 2. The elevations in Fig 1 show the configuration of the grain; it is worth noting that there has been no real attempt either to use or to match up halved or quartered veneers.

Mouldings

Both are cross-grained and would have been worked with moulding planes along the edge of a wide piece, being sawn off as strips of moulding afterwards. This has, almost inevitably, led to splits opening up across the grain.

Brasswork

The typical patterns of the period shown in the design for the Queen Anne style bureau-bookcase on page 98 apply equally well to this design.

Finish

A wax finish (see Appendix 5) would be most appropriate and should be applied over a sealing coat of shellac varnish.

Cutting List

	inches			mm		
	L	W	T	L	W	T
2 ends (A), each	23	17	¾	584	432	19
2 ends (B), each	17	17	¾	432	432	19
1 fall (C) as one piece	28	14	¾	711	356	19
1 top (D)	29	10	¾	737	254	19
2 shelves (E), each	28	16	¾	711	406	19
1 drawer division (F)	7	16	¾	178	406	19
1 top and 1 bottom (G), each	29	16½	¾	737	419	19
1 bottom (H)	28	15	⅝	711	381	16
1 well front (J)	28	4½	¾	711	114	19
1 panel (K)	28	13	⅜	711	330	10
1 upper back (L)	13	28	¼	330	711	6
1 lower back (LL)	23	28	¼	584	711	6
2 long rails (M), each	24	2	¾	609	51	19
2 end rails (N), each	10	2	¾	254	51	19
4 corner blocks (O), each	5	4½	¾	127	114	19
1 well back (P)	28	4	¾	711	102	19
2 rails (Q), each	29	2	¾	737	51	19
2 cross rails (R), each	13	2	¾	330	51	19
2 loper guides (S), each	13	3½	⅝	330	89	16
2 loper supports (T), each	15	3	¾	381	76	19
2 lopers (U), each	13	1⅛	¾	330	28	19

Drawer stuff

	L	W	T	L	W	T
2 top drawer fronts, each	13½	6½	¾	343	165	19
4 top drawer sides, each	16	6½	⅝	406	165	16
2 top drawer backs, each	13½	6½	⅜	343	159	10
2 top drawer bottoms, each	15	13½	¼	381	343	6
1 middle drawer front	27½	7½	¾	698	191	19
2 middle drawer sides, each	16	7½	⅝	406	191	16
1 middle drawer back	27½	7½	⅜	698	191	10
1 middle drawer bottom	15	27½	¼	381	698	6
1 bottom drawer front	27½	8	¾	698	203	19
2 bottom drawer sides, each	16	8	⅝	406	203	16
1 bottom drawer back	27½	8	⅜	698	203	10
1 bottom drawer bottom	15	27½	¼	381	698	6
8 drawer strips, each	14	1⅛	¼	356	28	6

Pigeonhole section

	L	W	T	L	W	T
4 end divisions, each	11	9¼	5/16	280	235	8
2 top shelves, each	6¼	5	5/16	159	127	8
2 middle shelves, each	9¼	5	5/16	235	127	8
2 drawer fronts, each	5¼	4	1¼	133	102	32
4 drawer sides, each	9	4	¼	228	102	6
2 drawer backs, each	5¼	4	¼	133	102	6
2 drawer bottoms, each	8½	5	3/16	216	127	5
3 long central divisions, each	11	5¼	¼	279	133	6
2 short central divisions, each	7	5¼	¼	178	133	6
1 central shelf, cuts 4	18	5¼	¼	457	133	6
2 central drawer fronts, each	8½	4	⅜	216	102	10
4 central drawer sides, each	5¼	4	¼	133	102	6
2 central drawer backs, each	8½	4	¼	216	102	6
2 central drawer bottoms, each	8½	5¼	3/16	216	133	5
1 top	27½	5½	5/16	698	140	8
1 bottom	27½	9¼	5/16	698	235	8
4 bun feet, each	4¾	4	–	121	102	–
Mouldings, one piece cuts all	96	1⅛	⅞	2438	29	22

Generous working allowances have been made to lengths and widths; thicknesses are net.

Queen Anne Style Bureau-Bookcase

A beautiful design that presents a challenge to the more accomplished cabinet maker. If made up in selected walnut it would certainly prove to be an eye-catching piece which would be the focus of attention in any room.

This piece is dated circa 1710 and is made in walnut, the fall and the drawer fronts being veneered in the same wood. The interior fitting consists of a stationery unit with pigeonholes and drawers (see Fig 1(A)), while the top drawer front is a dummy which encloses a well. Although not shown in the drawings, it would be a simple matter to cover the well with a lift-out panel, which could be lined with leather.

Its size, 6ft 6in by 3ft (1981mm by 915mm), should allow it to fit into most rooms, and the fact that the doors are plain-glazed and without bars helps to make it comparatively straightforward to construct. **Skill rating – 5.**

Bureau carcase

The top, bottom and sides are in solid walnut and are lap-dovetailed together. Good quality straight-grained English or European walnut is scarce and expensive and this means that you may have to consider an alternative. Man-made boards such as medium density fibre board (MDF), plywood or blockboard could be used but would need to be veneered on both sides and, in any case, it is difficult to cut neat dovetails in plywood or blockboard although it is possible in MDF. Sycamore would be an acceptable alternative timber and is about one-third the price of walnut; it mellows to a light golden brown which could easily be stained to resemble walnut.

Using a natural timber will almost certainly involve jointing two or more pieces together as described in Appendix 1. When marking out the ends (B) note that on each of them there is a small projection as shown in Fig 2 and this has to be allowed for – the size shown in the cutting list takes account of this. The back is pinned and glued into rebates worked on the back edges.

Bookcase

The two ends (C) are solid timber and are lap-dovetailed at their joints with the bottom piece (G) which is, of course, also solid.

At the top the two ends are mortise and tenoned into the rail (K) at the front and rail (L) at the back: similarly rail (M) is mortise and tenoned between the ends at the bottom. The latter two rails (L) and (M) are rebated at the back, as are the rear edges of the ends (C), so that the back can be pinned and glued in position.

The top moulding in Fig 1 is shown in profile in Fig 4(B), and can be glued and screwed in place, the corners being mitred. Glue blocks can be fixed to the inside of the framing around the top edges so that they support a drop-in top.

The shelf supports shown in Fig 2 are optional and while the pattern is true to period, doubtless there will be readers who would prefer to use one or other of the modern shelf fixings. A typical shelf is shown by the dashed lines in the end elevation in Fig 1.

Fig 3(A) shows a section through the closing stiles of the doors, which are conventional frames mortised and tenoned together.

Fig 1 Elevations, plan, and detail of the stationery unit.

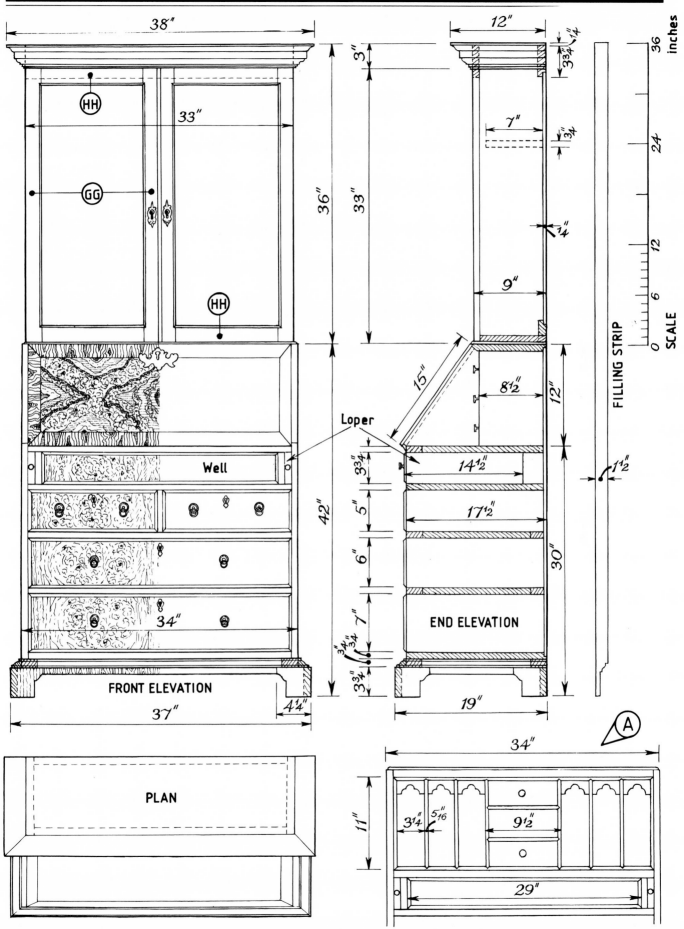

FRONT ELEVATION

END ELEVATION

FILLING STRIP

PLAN

Loper

Well

SCALE

inches

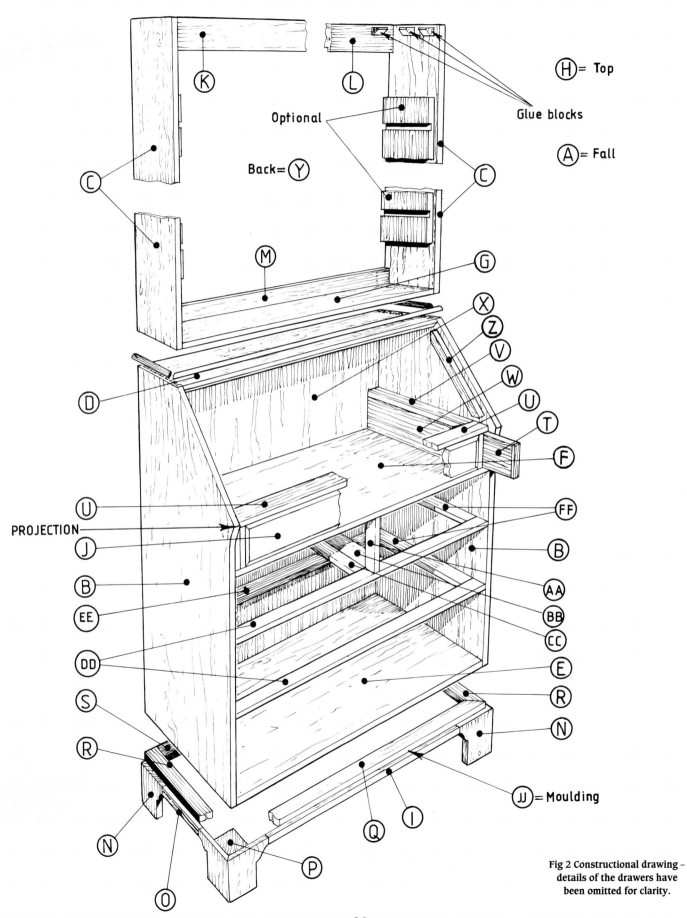

Fig 2 Constructional drawing –
details of the drawers have
been omitted for clarity.

Rebates need to be worked on the inner edges to accept the glass, which is held in place by fixing beads. The moulding worked on the inner edges is an optional feature; it can either be routed or worked by hand with a scratch-stock (Appendix 3). In any case you will need to cut what is known as a 'mason's mitre' at each corner, which consists of a mitre chiselled and shaped on the solid wood. There is also a cover beading pinned and glued into a small rebate made along the closing edge of the left-hand door when viewed from the front.

The bookcase stands loose on the bureau although it can be screwed down if you wish; moulding, (HH) Fig 2, is then pinned and glued around the front and ends.

Fall (*Fig 1 elevations and Fig 3(B)*)

This, more than any other part, needs to be stable and free from any tendency to shrink or warp as either fault would soon become glaringly obvious. If you can use suitable solid timber so much the better, but as the fall is veneered and crossbanded on the outside face and lined with leather on the inner, it would be feasible to utilize a man-made board. If so, it would be necessary to lip the edges as shown in Fig 3(B), the lipping being glued to the panel with a loose tongue; note that it would need to be rebated along the top and bottom edges.

The fall is hinged to part (U) in Fig 2 and rests against the strips (Z); the top front edge of the carcase (part D) has to be bevelled off as shown to accept the upper edge of the fall.

Laying leather linings is described in Appendix 6.

Drawers

These are of conventional construction with the fronts lap-dovetailed to the sides, Fig 4(E), and the grain of the drawer bottom running from front to back, as was usual for the period.

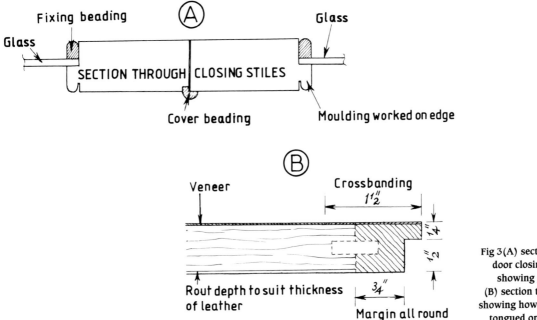

Fixing beading   (A)   Glass

Glass

SECTION THROUGH CLOSING STILES

Cover beading   Moulding worked on edge

(B)

Veneer   Crossbanding 1½"

Rout depth to suit thickness of leather   ¾"   Margin all round

Fig 3(A) section through the door closing stiles, also showing glass fixing; (B) section through the fall showing how a lipping can be tongued on it if required.

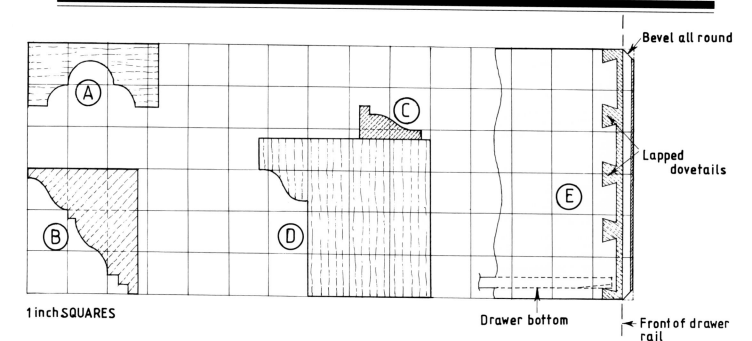

Bevel all round

Lapped dovetails

E

Drawer bottom

Front of drawer rail

1 inch SQUARES

Fig 4(A) detail of the arcaded pattern for the pigeonholes; (B) section of the top moulding (GG); (C) section of moulding (JJ); (D) profile of the plinth – note direction of grain; (E) section through one of the drawers.

A feature to note is that the edges of the drawer fronts are bevelled all round and stand proud of the carcase front (Fig 1 and Fig 4(E)); this protects the veneer on them from being damaged or splintered when the drawers are opened and closed.

From the point of view of historical authenticity, the drawer fronts should be made from best quality pine and the sides and bottoms from oak, but if good dry and knot-free pine is not available you could use sycamore as an alternative.

The topmost 'drawer front' (part (J), Fig 2) is in fact a dummy and, as already described, encloses a well which is revealed when the fall is opened. If desired, this well could be covered by a leather-lined loose panel which would rest on parts (U) and (V) in Fig 2, thus making a simple secret compartment.

Pigeonhole unit

This is shown at Fig 1 (A) and a detail at Fig 4 (A). The whole thing is self-contained and can be removed as a separate unit and replaced. This feature is found in many bureau-bookcases and secretaires of this and later periods, and in the days before banks and safe-deposits it enabled the owners to take important documents and ledgers with them on their travels.

It is made throughout in 5/16in (8mm) stuff, the divisions being vee-grooved and glued in place; the knobs on the drawers can be either brass or turned wood.

Fig 5 Suitable period patterns of escutcheons and drop-ring handles.

Lopers

These are pull-out bearers that support the fall when it is open, and details are shown in Fig 1 and also part (T), Fig 2.

Plinth

The four posts, part (P), Fig 2, to which the plinth facings (part (N) in Fig 2 and (D) in Fig 4) are glued and pocket-screwed (Appendix 1), are themselves screwed to a frame consisting of parts (Q), (R) and (S) – the front corners of this frame are mitred so that no end grain is visible. The carcase can then be located on to the frame and fixed, with the moulding (JJ) shown at Fig 4 (C) pinned and glued around the front and ends as shown at Fig 2.

Brasswork

Some typical designs of escutcheons and ring-drop handles are shown in Fig 5, and similar ones can be found in many modern catalogues. They can often be improved by filing a tiny bevel on their edges, being careful not to make it too regular (which would give a machine-produced look); a gentle rubbing with fine emery cloth also improves them.

Finish

This could be a spirit varnish as described in Appendix 5, or a shellac finish followed by a good quality wax polish applied from time to time.

Filling strip

This is optional and is a modern innovation to fill the gap between the back of the piece and the wall; it is, of course, scribed over the skirting board.

Cutting List

Part	inches L	W	T	mm L	W	T
1 fall (A)	34	15½	¾	863	394	19
2 bureau ends (B), each	39	19	¾	990	482	19
2 bookcase ends (C), each	34	9½	¾	863	241	19
1 bureau top (D)	35	10	¾	889	254	19
1 bureau bottom (E)	35	18	¾	889	457	19
1 bureau sub-top (F)	35	18	¾	889	457	19
1 bookcase bottom (G)	34	9½	¾	863	241	19
1 bookcase top (H)	33	9	¼	838	228	6
1 plinth front strip (I)	29½	1	¾	749	25	19
1 well front (J)	30	4¼	¾	762	108	19
1 bookcase top front rail (K)	34	4½	¾	863	114	19
1 bookcase top back rail (L)	34	4½	¾	863	114	19
1 bookcase bottom back rail (M)	34	2½	¾	863	64	19
8 plinth fronts (N), each	4½	4¾	¾	114	121	19
2 plinth end strips (O), each	11½	1	¾	292	25	19
4 plinth corner posts (P), each	4½	2½	2	114	64	51
1 plinth front rail (Q)	35	2¼	¾	889	57	19
2 plinth end rails (R), each	18	2¼	¾	457	57	19
1 plinth back rail (S)	33	2¼	¾	838	57	19
2 lopers (T), each	15½	4¼	¾	394	108	19
1 front rail (U)	34	2¼	¾	863	57	19
2 casing tops (V), each	17	2	¾	432	51	19
2 casing sides (W), each	17	4¼	¾	432	108	19
1 bureau back (X)	38	34	¼	965	863	6
1 bookcase back (Y)	33½	31	¼	851	787	6
2 support strips (Z), each	13	1½	¾	330	38	19
1 drawer muntin (AA)	7	2¼	¾	178	57	19

	in	in	in	mm	mm	mm
1 central drawer guide (BB)	15½	2¼	¾	394	57	19
1 central drawer runner (CC)	15½	4	¾	394	102	19
2 drawer rails (DD), each	34	2¼	¾	863	57	19
2 back rails (EE), each	34	2¼	¾	863	57	19
4 drawer runners (FF), each	15½	2¼	¾	394	57	19
1 top moulding, cuts all	66	3½	2¾	1676	89	70
1 bookcase moulding, cuts all	61	½	¼	1549	13	6
1 plinth moulding (JJ), cuts all	78	2¼	¾	1981	57	19

Door frames

	in	in	in	mm	mm	mm
4 stiles (GG), each	34	2¼	¾	863	57	19
4 rails (HH), each	15½	2¼	¾	394	57	19
1 cover bead	34	⅜	5/16	863	10	8
1 fixing glazing bead, cuts all	200	⅜	5/16	5080	10	8

Drawer stuff

	in	in	in	mm	mm	mm
2 upper fronts, each	17	5½	¾	432	140	19
1 middle front	33½	6½	¾	851	165	19
1 lower front	33½	7½	¾	851	191	19
4 upper sides, each	18	5½	⅜	457	140	10
2 middle sides, each	18	6½	⅜	457	165	10
2 lower sides, each	18	7½	⅜	457	191	10

	in	in	in	mm	mm	mm
2 upper backs, each	17	5½	⅜	432	140	10
1 middle back	33½	6½	⅜	851	165	10
1 lower back	33½	7½	⅜	851	191	10
2 upper drawer bottoms, each	18	17	¼	457	432	6
2 middle & lower drawer bottoms, each	18	33	¼	457	838	6

Pigeonhole unit

	in	in	in	mm	mm	mm
1 top & 1 bottom, each	33	9	5/16	838	228	8
2 ends, each	11½	9	5/16	292	228	8
6 vertical divisions, each	11½	9	5/16	292	228	8
2 drawer divisions, each	10	9	5/16	254	228	8
3 drawer fronts, each	9½	3¾	5/16	241	95	8
6 drawer sides, each	9	3¾	5/16	228	95	8
3 drawer bottoms, each	9	9½	5/16	228	241	8
1 back	11½	33	5/16	292	838	8

Optional parts

	in	in	in	mm	mm	mm
Shelves, each	32½	7½	¾	825	191	19
Filling strip (adapt sizes to suit)	79	2	⅜	2006	51	10
Shelf support rack – sizes to suit						

Note: Drawer rails finish 1⅞in by ¾in (48mm by 19mm).

Generous working allowances have been made to lengths and widths; thicknesses are net.

DRESSING MIRROR STAND

A comparatively plain design which should present no difficulties when being made up. Nevertheless, it possesses the elegant appearance that is a characteristic of the furniture from the reign of George IV.

This type of mirror first became popular in the mid-18th century when it was called a 'box toilet glass'; from the beginning of the 19th century it was commonly referred to as a 'dressing glass'. Our design is attributed to George Bullock, a London cabinet maker working in the 1820s and 30s, whose furniture has become greatly sought after during the past ten years. **Skill rating – 1.**

General remarks

The piece is veneered with pollarded oak and embellished with inlaid ebony bandings and lines – a combination of woods favoured by George Bullock. Pollarded oak comes from oak trees which have had their branches cut off at the 'poll' or crown; this tends to create burrs and curls in the grain, and the wood is now rare. You could substitute oak, walnut, or yew burr veneers but they are all difficult to lay; however, bird's eye maple or amboyna veneer would also give a good effect and is not so troublesome to work with.

Machining and construction

Bearing in mind that the outside of the carcase or box is completely veneered, the mitred joint is the only one that will not involve gluing on to any end grain and should therefore be used.

Fig 1 (A) constructional drawing; (B) how the woods are laminated.

DRAWER OMITTED FOR CLARITY

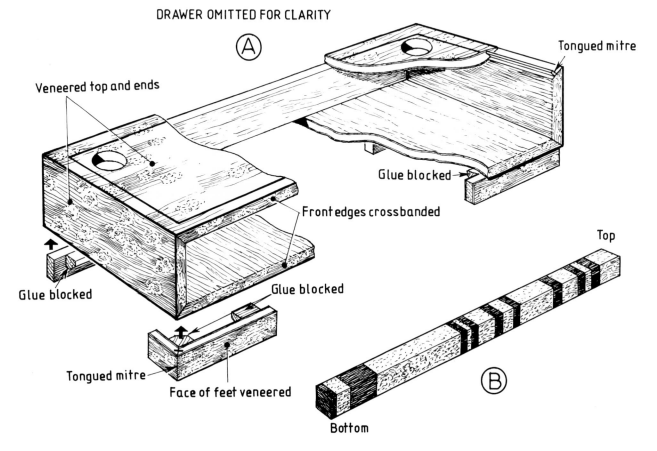

Veneered top and ends

Tongued mitre

Glue blocked

Front edges crossbanded

Glue blocked

Glue blocked

Tongued mitre

Face of feet veneered

Top

Bottom

(A) (B)

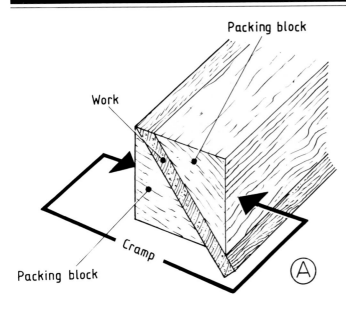

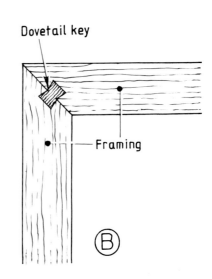

Fig 2(A) using cramping blocks to facilitate the working of a mitred edge; (B) how the dovetail key is inserted across a mitred joint.

The constructional drawing in Fig 1 shows mitred joints in which the faces are butted and glued together, the joints being reinforced by loose tongues. One good way to work the grooves for the tongues is to cut them on a table saw, most of which allow either the table or the saw to be tilted to 45 degrees; you may need to make one pass and then re-set the fence so that the second pass will make it slightly wider.

Alternatively, you could use a power router inverted to act like a spindle moulder. Packing blocks can be cramped (or stuck with double-sided adhesive tape) to the work piece as shown in Fig 2(A); they will not only form a bearing surface which will slide easily on the router table but will also make the work square so that you could still do the job on a table saw if you have one which does not tilt. Whichever method you employ, be careful to position the grooves so that they are located in the greatest depth of the wood – note also that the tongue should be cross-grained; a strip of plywood would be ideal.

The mirror frame also has mitred joints, each of which is strengthened by means of a small dovetail key let in as shown in Fig 2(B). The frames also need to be rebated as shown in Fig 3(E) to accept the mirror itself, which is held in place by beads pinned, not glued, so that they can be removed easily if the mirror needs to be replaced.

Ensuring that the turned pillars are rigidly fixed into the top is best done by making a sawcut in the bottom member, see Fig 3(F) and (H), so that a tiny wedge can be driven in when it is glued into the top; the small hole shown stops the sawcut from splitting too far. The pillars themselves are examples of laminated turnery where two different woods (or more) are glued together before being turned to give a decorative effect; in this case the woods are oak and ebony or whatever substitutes you have chosen. You can either glue the blanks end to end as in Fig 1(B), or make the pillar even stronger by incorporating loose pins glued in as shown by the dotted lines in Fig 3(H).

Fig 3(D) gives details of the drawer and this follows the

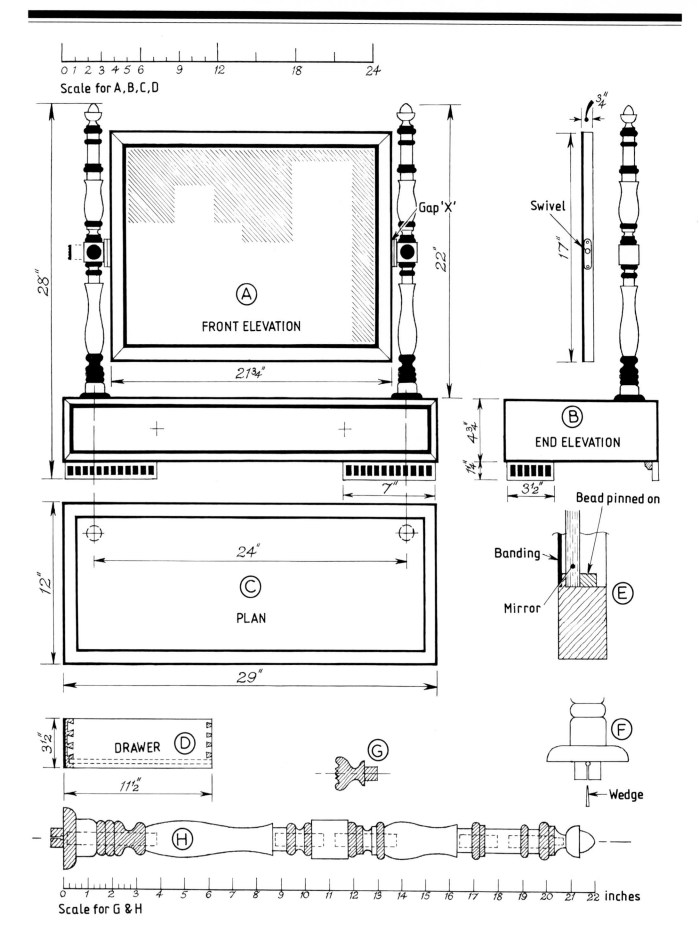

Scale for A, B, C, D
0 1 2 3 4 5 6   9   12   18   24

Gap 'X'

28"

22"

21¾"

Ⓐ FRONT ELEVATION

¾"

Swivel

17"

Ⓑ END ELEVATION

4¾"

1¼"

3½"

7"

12"

24"

Ⓒ PLAN

29"

Bead pinned on

Banding

Mirror

Ⓔ

3½"

DRAWER Ⓓ

11½"

Ⓖ

Ⓕ

Wedge

Ⓗ

Scale for G & H
0 1 2 3 4 5 6 7 8 9 10 11 12 13 14 15 16 17 18 19 20 21 22 inches

orthodox construction. The back of the box can be pocket-screwed and glued to the underside of the top, and screwed to the bottom from underneath; the feet are glue-blocked to the bottom of the box as shown in Fig 1(A).

Veneering

As already mentioned, the box is veneered all over using the methods described in Appendix 2, and the technique of laying bandings and lines is dealt with in Appendix 3.

Fittings

The only metal fittings are those between the pillars and the mirror frame, and the pattern shown appears to be obsolete and consequently unobtainable. These days there is an alternative known as a 'mirror pivot', which is stocked by most retailers, and you will need a pair of them. In the front elevation of Fig 3 there is an annotation 'Gap X'; this is to warn you that it is advisable to buy the fittings first as they may vary slightly in size and thickness from one maker to another, before marking out the holes for the pillars.

Finish

The spirit varnish described in Appendix 5 would be an appropriate finish, although one of the modern synthetic lacquers would best suit those who do not need historical authenticity as they are proof against the various chemicals used in modern cosmetics.

Cutting List

	inches			mm		
	L	W	T	L	W	T
1 top and 1 bottom, each	30	5¼	⅝	762	133	16
2 ends, each	13	5¼	⅝	330	133	16
4 feet, each	7½	1¾	⅝	191	45	16
1 back	29	5	½	736	127	13
2 pillars, ebony, each	8	1¾	1½	203	45	38
2 pillars, oak, each	16½	1¾	1½	419	45	38
1 drawer front	29	4	½	736	102	13
2 drawer sides, each	12	4	⅜	305	102	10
1 drawer back	29	3½	⅜	736	89	10
1 drawer bottom	29	12	¼	736	305	6
2 mirror frame stiles, each	18	1½	¾	457	38	19
2 mirror frame rails, each	23	1½	¾	584	38	19

Generous working allowances have been made to lengths and widths; thicknesses are net.

AMERICAN HIGH-POST BED

*Called a 'four poster' in Britain
today, a term which may suggest
something heavy and luxurious clad
in voluminous drapery. However, from
such earlier designs developed light and
elegant versions, like this one from
North America.*

In Britain these are called 'tent beds' or 'field beds' – the terms are interchangeable – as they could be dismantled easily when they were used in medieval times by travellers, or by high-ranking officers on military campaigns. In the 17th and 18th centuries they became more elaborate and were often used by the aristocracy on their travels in preference to frequently verminous hotel beds. Later still, in the 19th century, the fact that they could be taken apart was an advantage when moving house.

In some designs the tester rails around the top frame had to support a heavy canopy and curtains which were needed to keep out draughts, but on the one illustrated here the canopy was a light one made of lace, purely for decoration. This particular style was popular from the late 18th century until the middle of the 19th and it is difficult to date our example precisely, but the fact that the bedding is supported on ropes (called 'bed lines') indicates a date at the end of the 18th century. In later designs the bedding was supported by a sheet of ticking laced to the bed rails, or a metal mesh.

The bed is in mahogany throughout; alternatively a strong, straight-grained timber such as beech could be used for the posts, the frame, and the tester rails, although an attractively figured panel of solid mahogany or walnut is required for the headboard, which is a show piece. **Skill rating – 3.**

Posts

Only the two posts at the foot of the bed are turned, and their length means that they have to be turned in sections that will fit your woodturning lathe; the dotted lines on the detail of these columns in Fig 1 suggest suitable lengths. Although a pin turned on the head of one section can be glued into a hole bored in the end of the next one to provide a satisfactory joint, it would be much better if the pin and its matching socket could be threaded so that they could be screwed together dry and not glued. This necessitates using a screwbox and tap (which have made a welcome reappearance after several years' absence); many woodturners have at least one and find it invaluable.

Whichever method you use it is advisable to make the pins and their sockets before turning the main parts as this will ensure that the sections match perfectly afterwards. Note that the squares into which the rails are tenoned have their ends pummelled off in the lathe, although it is not essential.

The posts at the head of the bed are 2¼in (57mm) square to the height of the side rail and then taper to 1¼in (32mm) at the upper end; the corners are planed off to give an octagonal cross section as shown in Fig 1.

Working the reeding on the turned posts

This is tricky and needs to be done carefully; Fig 2 (A) shows what is probably the safest way to do it, although not the quickest. At

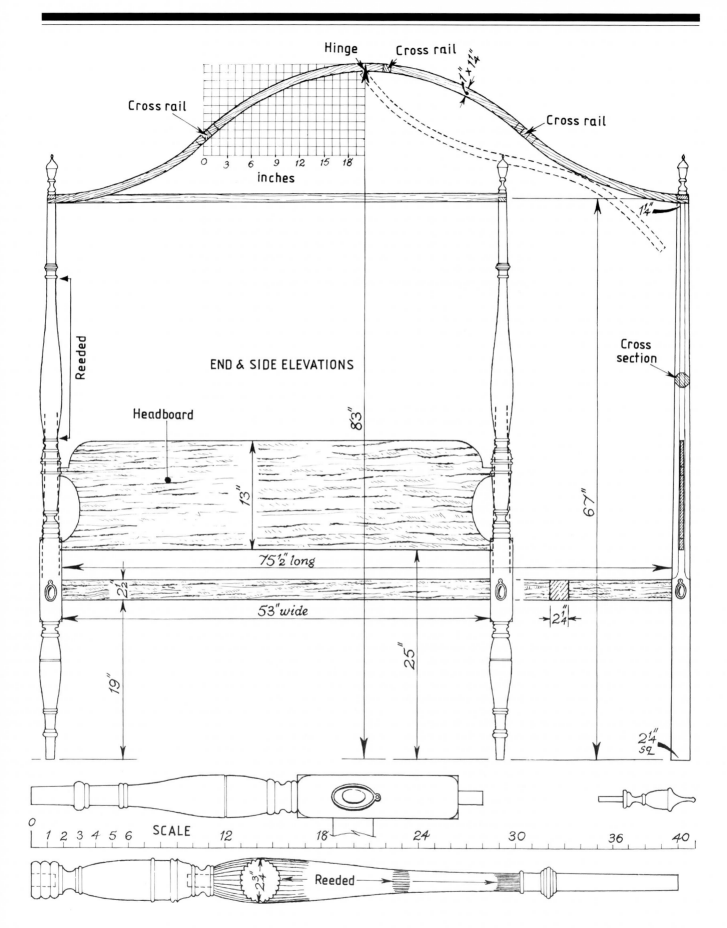

Hinge

Cross rail

1" × 1¼"

Cross rail

Cross rail

Cross rail

1¼"

0 3 6 9 12 15 18

inches

Reeded

Cross section

END & SIDE ELEVATIONS

Headboard

83"

13"

67"

75½" long

2½"

53" wide

2¼"

25"

19"

2¼" sq

SCALE

0 1 2 3 4 5 6   12   18   24   30   36   40

2¾"

Reeded

Fig 1 Elevations and diagram
of the turned parts.

first glance it may appear that the power router is ideal for the job but unfortunately the sole plate is usually too large to negotiate the curves, whereas the scratch-stock illustrated at (B) will take them in its stride.

The first step is to make the cradle which has its upper edges shaped to match the curves of the post exactly; the ends have U-shaped slots cut out for the work to rest in snugly, and blocks should be provided for cramping it down tightly.

Obviously some kind of indexing method is needed so that the twenty-four reeds can be marked out accurately. This can be done by drawing a semicircle of 1⅜in (35mm) radius on a piece of thick white cardboard and dividing it by means of a protractor into twelve equal parts of 15 degrees. Extend the marks by ½in (13mm) or so beyond the circumference and cut round the latter so that when the card is held vertically against the work and on the register marks (which are at its greatest diameter) a pair of the

Fig 2(A) the set-up for working the reeds; (B) details of the scratch-stock; (C) interlacing the bed lines; (D) a suspension cabinet fitting can be used with ledge rails for a plywood or chipboard base.

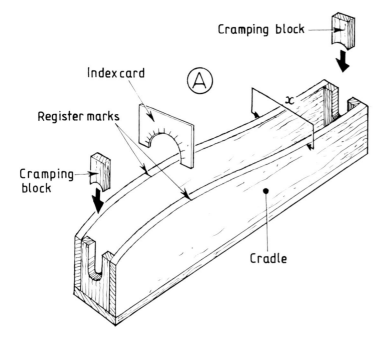

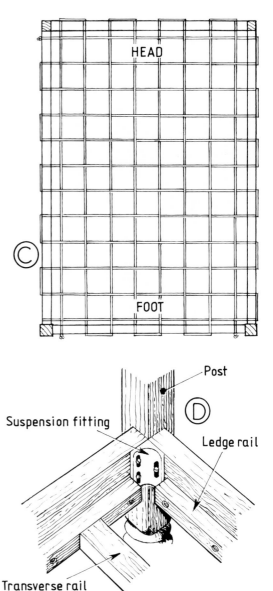

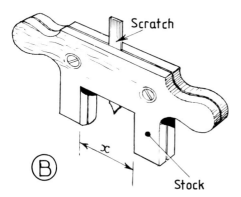

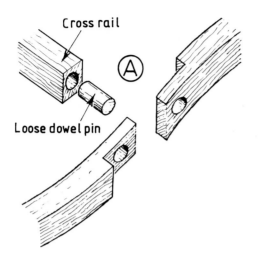

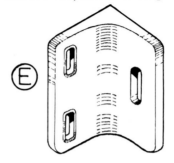

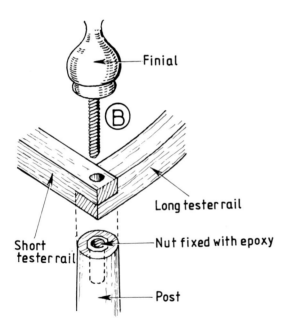

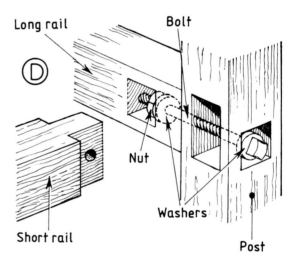

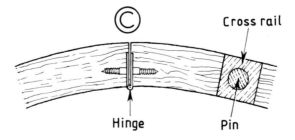

Fig 3(A) the joint between a cross rail and a curved tester rail; (B) the halved joint at the corners; (C) detail of the hinge at the centre of the curved tester rails; (D) how the frame rails are connected at the corners; (E) a cabinet suspension fitting.

reeds can be marked. By rotating the work, the next pair can be marked and so on.

Fig 2 (B) shows a suitable scratch-stock which can be sawn from a piece of scrap timber and then split into matching halves as described in Appendix 3; the important point is that the two dimensions marked '*x*' are equal and such that the stock will slide smoothly along the cradle.

Tester rails

These are quite slender – 1 in (25mm) thick by 1¼in (32mm) wide – as they are not intended to support heavy drapery but only a lace cover or something similar. An unusual feature is that the long rails are hinged in the middle as shown in Fig 1 and Fig 3 (C) so that they can be folded back on one another when the bed has to be dismantled, and this is indicated by the dotted line in Fig 1. The fact that the serpentine curve is a regular ogee not only enables this to be done, but also means that the rails can be cut from one solid piece and nested when marking them out; this avoids any steam-bending. Each section of the rail is joined by a halving joint at its centre, and a cross rail is glued to this by means of a loose dowel pin which penetrates the joint and reinforces it (see Fig 3 (A)).

At each corner the two rails are again connected by a halving joint, although this one is not glued but left dry as in Fig 3 (B); the threaded shank of the finial is screwed through the joint into a nut which is fixed with epoxy adhesive into a hole bored in the end of the post. The finials can be either wood or brass, and Charles Greville (see Suppliers' List on page 158) have a wide selection of the latter.

Frame

Assuming that you want to reproduce the bed in its original form, you will need very stout frame rails – 2¼in (58mm) square – as the rope mattress precludes having any transverse rails because of the possibility of its sagging on to them.

The method of connecting the rails and posts so that they can be taken apart is shown in Fig 3 (D). At each corner a bed bolt is inserted through a hole bored through the post and into another bored in the end of the long rail; on the way it also penetrates a hole bored through the tenon on the end of the short rail. Each bolt needs to be 5 to 6in long (127 to 153mm) and ⅜ to ½in diameter (10 to 13mm); it helps if the nut is square so that it can be gripped easily while the bolt is tightened up. Two stout heavy washers are also required to provide good bearing surfaces.

Adapting the bed to carry a modern base and mattress is quite straightforward, and the fitting shown at Fig 3 (E) is worth consideration. It is actually a suspension fitting for cabinets but it would be a good choice for screwing or bolting the frame rails to the posts; incidentally each fitting can support over 260lb (120kg).

Headboard

This is a panel which is shaped as shown in Fig 1, the four tongues being mortised into the head posts. It is the part of the bed that really catches the eye and consequently the grain or figuring needs to be decorative. Because of its curved outline it would be difficult to use a veneered man-made board as this would have to be lipped round, and a solid panel is more practical.

Springing

As illustrated in Fig 2(C), the springing on the original bed consists of a web of interlaced lengths of rope called 'bed lines' which are inserted through holes bored along the centre line of the frame rails.

It is more likely that you will want to use a modern sprung mattress; if so there are two choices of springing to support it, namely either resilient rubber webbing or a sheet of multi-plywood which rests on the ledge rails shown in Fig 2(D). In the case of the webbing, a couple of transverse rails would be needed to counteract the considerable tension it exerts, and similar rails could be used to help in supporting the plywood base.

Brasswork

You will need eight brass cover plates to hide the heads of the bolts – four of them are only dummies to maintain symmetry. The nearest modern equivalents are cylinder lock covers obtainable from H. E. Savill (see Suppliers' List).

Finish

The shellac varnish described in Appendix 5 would be the most appropriate.

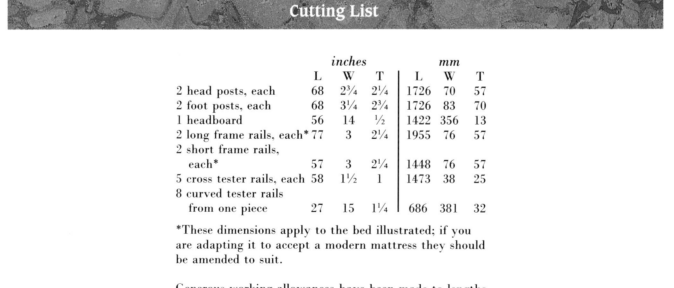

Cutting List

	inches			*mm*		
	L	W	T	L	W	T
2 head posts, each	68	2¾	2¼	1726	70	57
2 foot posts, each	68	3¼	2¾	1726	83	70
1 headboard	56	14	½	1422	356	13
2 long frame rails, each*	77	3	2¼	1955	76	57
2 short frame rails, each*	57	3	2¼	1448	76	57
5 cross tester rails, each	58	1½	1	1473	38	25
8 curved tester rails from one piece	27	15	1¼	686	381	32

*These dimensions apply to the bed illustrated; if you are adapting it to accept a modern mattress they should be amended to suit.

Generous working allowances have been made to lengths and widths; thicknesses are net.

BONHEUR DU JOUR

This is the kind of small table that the French ébénistes delighted in producing; its elegance and usefulness soon made it as popular in the England of the late 18th century as in France.

A s its name implies, this kind of small table originated in France, first appearing about 1760 and being introduced into Britain in the last twenty years of the 18th century. The design shown dates from about 1780. It is made in mahogany with satinwood inlays and stringing, and the crossbanding on the writing surface of the fall flap is tulipwood. **Skill rating – 3.**

General description

Basically the design is a small writing table and incorporates a fold-over flap which, when opened, rests upon the drawer which is pulled out to act as a support. The cupboards and drawers not only act as storage for stationery and writing materials but could also be subdivided to hold jewellery and trinkets.

Legs (*part A, Fig 2*)

These are tapered and are made following the method described in the design for a serpentine-fronted sideboard on page 54. The easiest way to work the collars near the foot of each leg is to cut and shape them first as small separate blocks, four to each leg, and pin and glue them in place once the legs have been tapered.

The recesses for the inlays can be routed out but a good method is to cut round the outlines first with a craft knife, following with a sharp narrow chisel so that a narrow border of (say) ¼in (6mm) wide and as deep as the thickness of the veneer is worked along the inside of the outlines. The sharp corners have to be cut by hand as the cutter of a power router will leave them rounded; this way you can remove the remainder of the wood using the power router freehand, thus avoiding the need for a template.

Frame

From Fig 2, you will see that sockets have to be chopped out of the tops of the front legs to accept the dovetail pins worked on the ends of the upper drawer rail (B). In addition, a horizontal mortise has to be cut to accept the tenon on each end of the lower drawer rail, which is also marked (B).

The end and back rails, (C) and (D), are jointed to the legs with double tenons as shown; the remainder of the frame rails, namely parts (E) and (F), are mortised and tenoned into the legs. Note that part (F) is extra wide to act as a drawer runner as well as a frame rail; the drawer guide (G) can be pinned and glued in place.

Top, panel and cabinet base
(*parts H, K and L, Fig 2*)

These are all solid wood, although they may have to be jointed as described in Appendix 1 to make up the requisite widths.

There should be no difficulty in hingeing the flap to the top as it simply involves screwing two solid brass 1¾in (45mm) or 2in (51mm) hinges to the edges, making sure that the flaps are sunk

Fig 1 Elevations and plans.

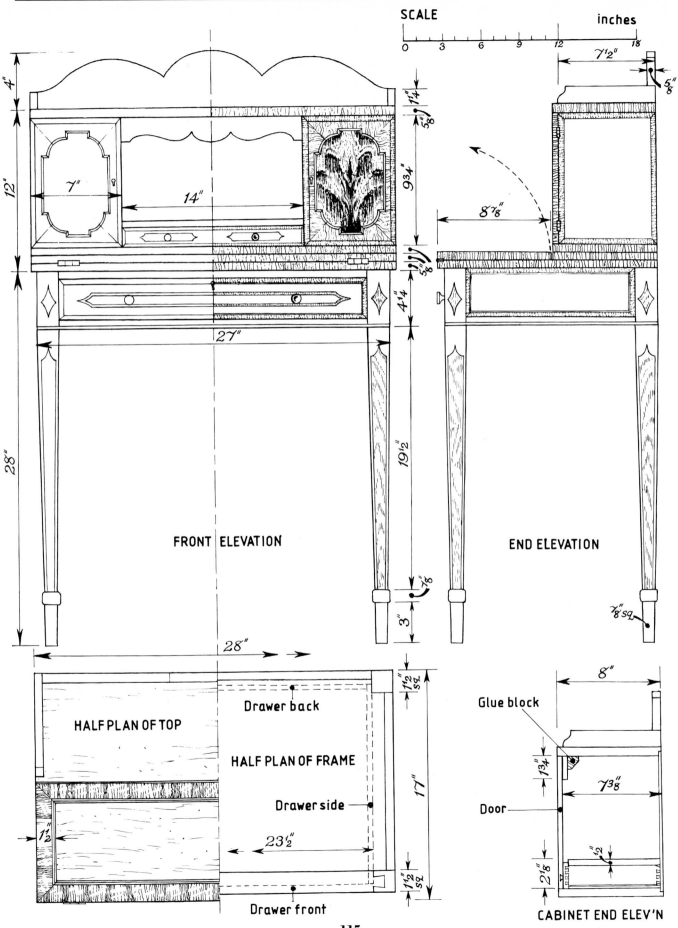

SCALE   inches

FRONT ELEVATION

END ELEVATION

HALF PLAN OF TOP

HALF PLAN OF FRAME

Drawer back

Drawer side

Drawer front

Glue block

Door

CABINET END ELEV'N

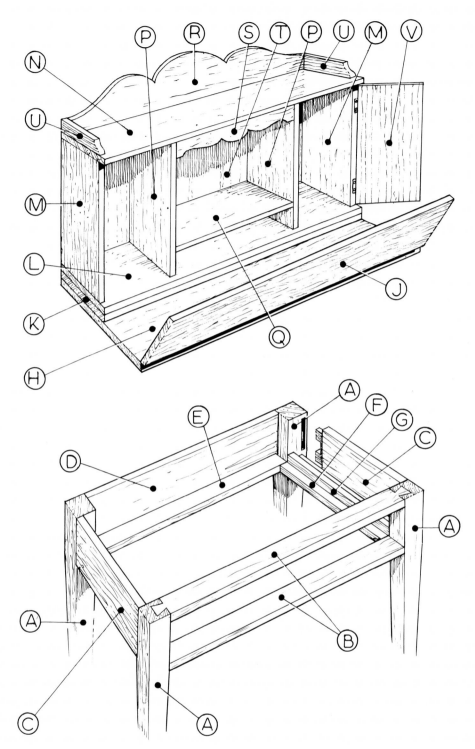

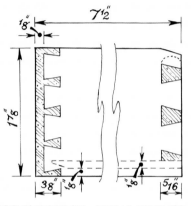

SIDE ELEVATION - SMALL DRAWER

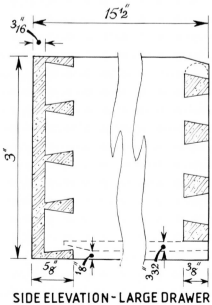

SIDE ELEVATION - LARGE DRAWER

Fig 2 Drawings showing
construction, plus elevations of
large and small drawers.

flush on each. Part (K) can be glued and screwed to (H), and the screws will need to be well countersunk.

Cabinet

As all the parts are, again, solid wood the base (L), the ends (M), and the top (N) can be mortise and tenoned together – double tenons as already described would be most effective.

The vertical divisions (P) and the shelf (Q) can be stop-housed into position (see Appendix 1) and assembly made easy by first of all gluing them and then pushing them home from the back. The small fascia (S) can be glue-blocked in place as shown in the cabinet end elevation in Fig 1; and the easiest way to deal with the gallery pieces is to dowel them on to the cabinet top. Their shapes are set out in Fig 3(B) and (E) and as they are shown as half elevations you will need to plot the matching halves from the squared-off drawing.

The doors are the 'lay-on' type and each one can be fixed with two solid brass hinges measuring 1in by ⅝in (25mm by 16mm) with the flaps recessed into the edge of part (M) and the door (V). The back (T) is glued and pinned into rebates worked on the back edges.

Drawers

Fig 2 shows details of these in elevation and they are made in the conventional manner, with the bottoms grooved into the sides and the back of the drawer front. When this method of fixing the drawer bottoms is adopted, you must ensure that the lowest dovetail is wide enough to accommodate the groove; it often helps if the front edge of the bottom is tapered off, as shown.

You will need to pin and glue small blocks to the lower drawer rail (B) and position them so that they engage with similar blocks fixed to the underside of the large drawer bottom; this will stop the drawer being withdrawn completely when it is acting as a support.

Veneering

This is the most time-consuming job of all and although veneering is discussed in Appendices 2 and 3, the following notes should make things clearer.

Marking out the patterns on the doors is likely to give the most trouble as it must be done perfectly, otherwise the slightest defect will be only too obvious. Fig 3(A) shows the setting out on a grid of 1in (25mm) squares; the central cartouche as shown in the front elevation in Fig 1 is in mahogany veneer and calls for something dramatic in the way of figure. The corners and crossbanded borders are in satinwood, as are the ⅛in (3mm) stringings and the crossbandings on the drawers, plus the crossbandings shown on the end elevation in Fig 1.

Grooving out the channels for the stringings can be done with a power router fitted with a ⅛in (3mm) cutter or by hand with a scratch-stock; in any case the chevron shapes at the ends will need to be cut by hand as well, first along the edges with a craft knife and then finished with a narrow ⅛in (3mm) chisel.

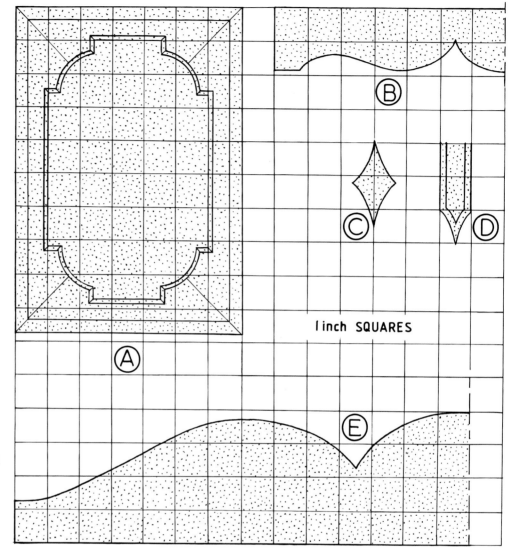

Fig 3 One inch squared-off
drawing showing (A) veneered
pattern of door; (B) half
elevation of fascia;
(C) diamond shape at top of
legs; (D) chevron pattern;
(E) half elevation of
gallery back.

1 inch SQUARES

All exterior edges in the actual piece are cross-veneered; and this does make it easier to use veneered plywood or medium density fibre board (MDF) if you are not concerned with authenticity, as the edges will be covered.

Brasswork

In addition to the hinges which have already been described, the only other fittings are the flat circular knobs for the drawers which are widely available, and the three locks comprising a brass cut-drawer lock and two brass cut-link plate cupboard locks for the doors. The latter need not be handed as the bolt shoots either right or left; the lock itself is recessed flush into the inside of the door and the striking plate is let into the front edge. If you find this type difficult to obtain, an alternative is a plain straight cupboard lock which is not let in but simply screwed on to the inside of the door; you will need two, as they are right and left handed.

Finish

The most appropriate is the traditional shellac finish described in Appendix 5.

Cutting List

	inches			mm		
	L	W	T	L	W	T
4 legs (A), each	30	2	1½	762	51	38
2 drawer rails (B), each	28	1⅞	⅝	711	48	11
2 end panels (C), each	17	4¾	⅝	432	121	11
1 back panel (D)	28	4¾	⅝	711	121	11
1 back frame rail (E)	28	1⅞	⅝	711	48	11
2 drawer runners (F), each	17	2½	⅝	432	64	11
2 drawer guides (G), each	15	1	⅝	381	25	11
1 top (H)	29	17½	⅝	737	445	11
1 fall flap (J)	29	9½	⅝	737	241	11
1 intermediate panel (K)	29	8½	⅝	737	216	11
1 cabinet base (L)	29	8½	⅝	737	216	11
2 cabinet ends (M), each	11¼	8	⅝	286	203	11
1 cabinet top (N)	29	8½	⅝	737	216	11
2 cabinet divisions (P), each	10¾	8	⅝	273	203	11
1 shelf (Q)	15	8	⅝	381	203	11
1 gallery back (R)	29	4½	⅝	737	115	11
1 fascia (S)	15	2½	⅝	381	64	11
1 cabinet back (T)	27	11	¼	686	279	6
2 gallery ends (U), each	8	1⅝	⅝	203	42	11
2 cabinet doors (V), each	10½	7½	⅝	267	190	11
Drawers						
1 large drawer front	24½	3½	⅝	622	89	11
2 large drawer sides, each	16	3½	⅜	407	89	10
1 large drawer back	24½	3¼	⅜	622	83	10
1 large drawer bottom	16	24½	³⁄₃₂	407	622	2.4
1 small drawer front	14½	2⅜	⅜	368	60	10
2 small drawer sides, each	8	2⅜	⁵⁄₁₆	203	60	8
1 small drawer back	14½	2¼	⁵⁄₁₆	368	57	8
1 small drawer bottom	8	14½	⅛	203	368	3

Generous working allowances have been made to lengths and widths; thicknesses are net.

LINEN CHEST

*This kind of chest was usually found
in a bedroom at the foot of the bed; it is
as useful today as ever it was for
storing linen, blankets, and the like.
It would make a handsome and
original gift for any young
newlyweds.*

Historically there were three distinct styles of this kind of chest, each more sophisticated than the one before. Before the 13th century 'dug-out' chests were used and, as the name implies, consisted of baulks of solid timber which had hollow compartments hewn out of them. During the 13th and 14th centuries they were made up of boards or planks nailed together, and by the 15th century 'joined' chests with framed-up panels as shown here were being produced. **Skill rating – 3.**

General remarks

Our design, which dates back to the early 17th century, is made in oak as was most vernacular furniture of the period, but other local timbers such as ash, beech, chestnut and elm were used as well depending on what ready-sawn timber was available. If you are not concerned with historical accuracy, try making it in ash. It is easily obtainable, reasonably inexpensive, and often resembles oak so closely that only an expert can tell the difference. If you are leaving the panels plain, they could consist of medium density fibre board (MDF) or plywood veneered with oak on the outside and a balancer on the inside (see Appendix 2).

Chests were normally specially built for a particular customer by the local joiner, often to celebrate a betrothal or a wedding, and the standards of workmanship and methods of construction vary considerably. Some pieces have the backs nailed on, and possibly the bottom as well; and there were several ways of fixing the panels and hingeing the lid.

Construction

This is shown in the lower drawing of Fig 1, and all of the joints on the rails, corner posts and muntins are draw-bore mortised and tenoned, a type of joint explained in Appendix 1. They can be framed up dry, as most of them were, because the glues of the period were notoriously unreliable. The panels must in any case be inserted dry so that they are free to shrink or swell to accommodate any changes in humidity. They are 'fielded' on the inside edges (see Fig 2(A)), which allows them to be thick enough for the depth of the decorative carving.

The lid will almost certainly have to comprise two pieces unless you are lucky enough to have a single board of the requisite width. You can, of course, rub-joint these together but it would be more in period to use cleats as shown at Fig 4 (*left*); the screws or nails should be inserted through slots in the cleats which, as explained in Appendix 1, will allow any movement caused by shrinkage to take place.

The bottom boards have the grain running from back to front and are slot-screwed up into rebates on the lower edges of the frame, although they would originally have been nailed which inevitably led to splitting in many old pieces. Many chests contained a small tray similar to the one shown in Fig 2(B) which held

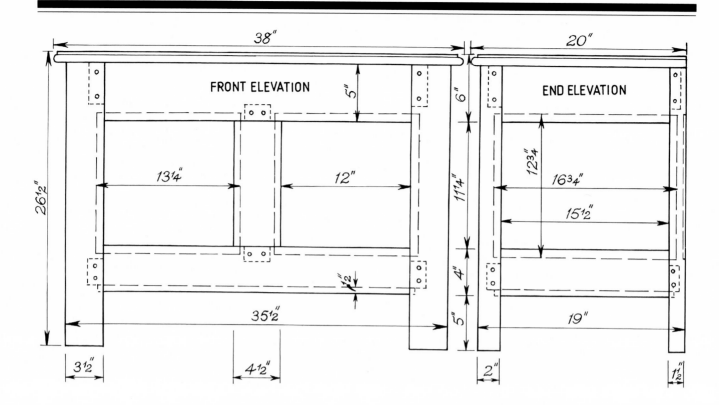

FRONT ELEVATION

END ELEVATION

38"

20"

26½"

5"

6"

11¼"

13¼"

12"

12¾"

16¾"

15½"

4"

1½"

5"

35½"

19"

3½"

4½"

2"

1½"

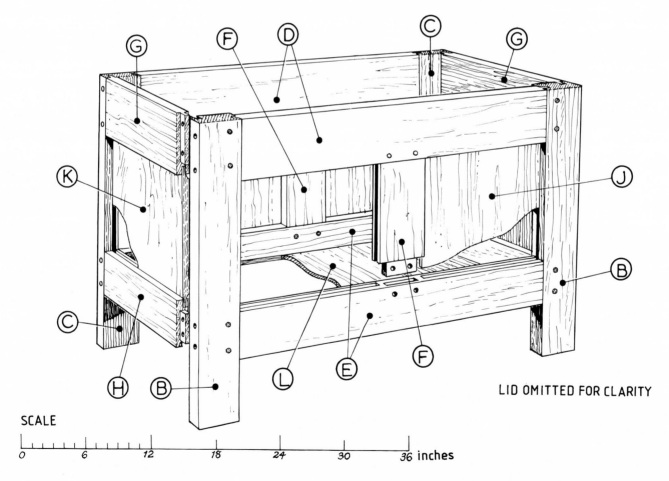

LID OMITTED FOR CLARITY

SCALE

0   6   12   18   24   30   36 inches

Fig 1 Front and end elevations;
drawing showing construction.

fragrant herbs such as lavender which would scent the linen. The tray can be either a fixture at one end or (as shown) supported by strips that run the whole length so that it could be slid along to any desired position.

Decoration

This is very much a matter of personal preference and you may decide to leave the chest quite plain except for chamfering the edges of the rails around the panels.

Fig 3 shows details of the various patterns superimposed on a grid of 1in (25mm) squares, and if you decide to carve them bear in mind that accuracy is not so important as the spirit and spontaneity of the design. Almost certainly the carving on the original was done by a joiner who had the knack for that kind of work, and it is interesting to note that in 1632 the London Court of Aldermen decreed that joiners should be allowed to undertake wood carving; the result has a pleasant appearance without being too exact and formal.

It is unlikely that you will have the hundred or so chisels and gouges that make up a professional's set of carving tools, but the

Fig 2(A) detail of fielding on panel; (B) sketch of tray; (C) strap hinge; (D) typical hasp lock.

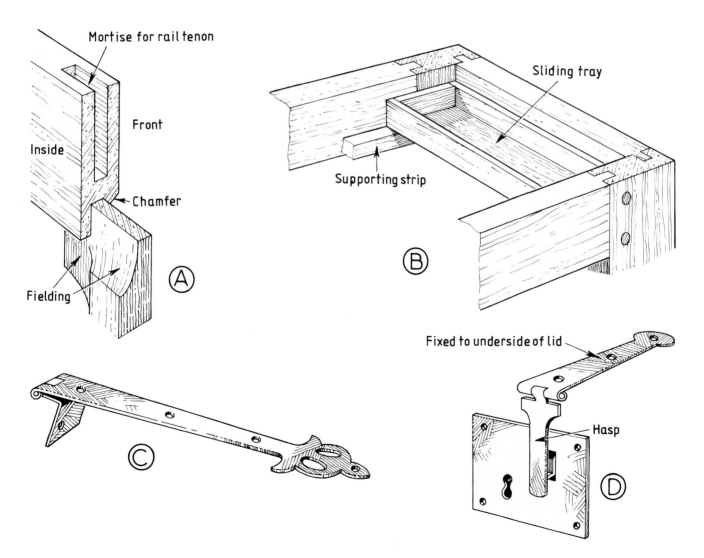

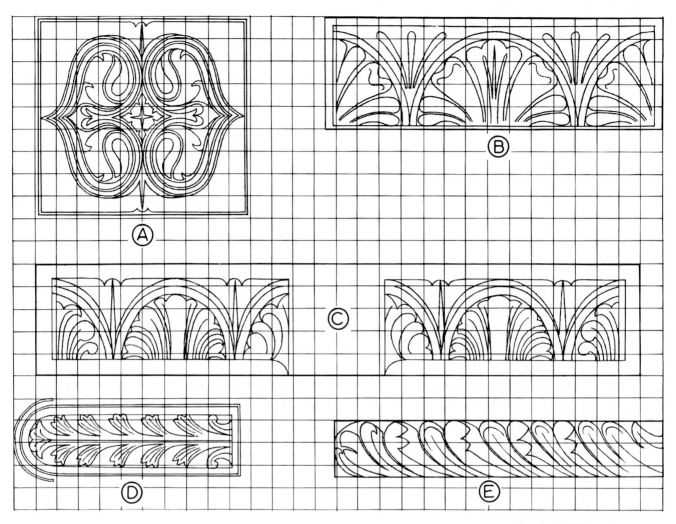

One inch (25mm) squares

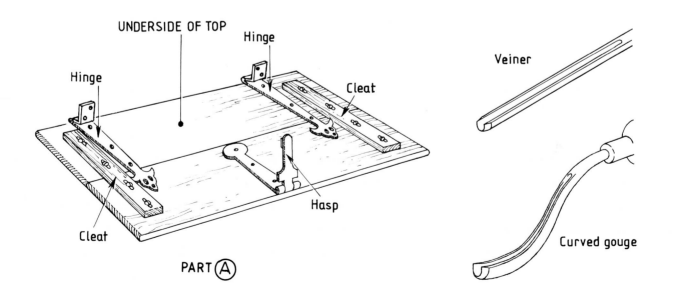

UNDERSIDE OF TOP

Hinge

Hinge

Cleat

Hasp

Cleat

PART Ⓐ

Veiner

Curved gouge

Fig 3 Decorative patterns of
(A) panels; (B) end rail;
(C) top rail; (D) muntin;
(E) post.

two gouges shown in Fig 4 (*right*) which are a ⅛in (3mm) veiner and a ¼in (6mm) curved gouge, should enable you to be reasonably successful. The designs also lend themselves very readily to being routed by a power router if you do not mind working freehand – the finer details could then be applied with standard cabinet chisels and gouges afterwards.

Metalwork

Cranked strap hinges, as in Fig 2(C), are used to hinge the lid and they are still a standard hinge today. Unfortunately they are usually finished in black japan which looks rather incongruous, but the finish could be stripped off to expose the steel beneath.

The hasp lock shown in Fig 2(D) was widely used during the 17th century but has long since been obsolete; those who require historical accuracy can only hope to find a metalworker who will make one specially – the same remarks also apply to the hinges. The modern equivalent would be a box lock or a till lock.

Finish

This could be either a linseed oil, or a wax finish; both are described in Appendix 5.

Cutting List

	inches			mm		
	L	W	T	L	W	T
2 pieces for top (A), each	40	21	1	1016	533	25
2 front posts (B), each	26½	4	2	673	102	21
2 back posts (C), each	26½	4	1½	673	102	38
2 top rails (D), each	32½	5½	1½	825	140	38
2 bottom rails (E), each	32½	4½	1½	825	115	38
2 muntins (F), each	15½	5	1½	394	127	38
2 top end rails (G), each	18½	5	1½	470	127	38
2 bottom end rails (H), each	18½	4½	1½	470	115	38
4 front and back panels (J), each	14	13½	⅝	356	343	16
2 end panels (K), each	17½	13½	⅝	445	343	16
1 bottom board (L)	18	31	½	457	787	13
Tray and cleats extra, if required						

Generous working allowances have been made to lengths and widths; thicknesses are net.

Fig 4 (left) sketch of underside of lid; (right) suggested gouges for carving.

LIVERY CUPBOARD

Not a piece for the faint-hearted to make up! In the proper setting this cupboard would endow its surroundings with the sturdy attractiveness of much of the furniture from the early 1600s and also provide useful storage space in the dining room.

This piece dates back to the early 17th century and is similar to a court cupboard except that the latter does not have the small 'hutch' or cupboard in the upper stage. Originally a 'cupboard' was, as the name implies, a board on which plate and drinking vessels were displayed – the greater the number of boards (more properly called 'stages'), the higher the owner's status in society. A court cupboard has three open shelves, one above the other, and is rarely much taller than about 48in (1220mm). (The adjective 'court' relates to the French for 'short' and has no royal connotations.) 'Livery' refers to the allowance of food and drink customarily given to guests and servants, left in their rooms to sustain them through the long winter nights. **Skill rating** – 5.

General description

Oak is by far the most appropriate timber for making up the design, although elm boards could be used for the top, the middle stage, and the pot board; the top in the original piece is rather flimsy and has been replaced by thicker ¾in (19mm) timber to provide additional strength.

As is the case with the linen chest on page 120, if you are hoping to achieve an antique appearance it is best not to be too precise in the construction as nothing looks more out of place than machine-cut hairline joints on a supposedly period piece; by the same token it is better to use random width boards for the parts so described in the cutting list.

Construction

As you can see from the elevations in Fig 1 and the constructional diagram in Fig 2, all the mortised and tenoned joints are draw-bored as described in Appendix 1. The two boards that comprise the top can be nailed down with their heart sides opposed if you have antique nails, otherwise oak dowels or pegs can be employed to do the job. The same remarks apply to the boards (part (N)) on the middle stage and those on the pot board, part (O), see Fig 2, page 129.

Many of the old pieces had the back boards simply nailed on, but in this design the boards are pinned into rebates worked on parts (B), (E) and (J) of the back frame. The pulvinated frieze is more usually called a 'cushion frieze' and is pinned to the rails (G) and (K), the heads of the pins being punched below the surface and filled; obviously the pins should be driven in where the carved pattern will help to make them inconspicuous, at least to casual observation.

Turning now to the cupboard section which is shown in detail in the plan in Fig 1, note that the rails and stiles are much thicker than normal to allow for the fixing of the chamfered mouldings which are pinned to them. Fig 1 (A) shows a plan section through a rail. The panels themselves are also thicker so that the recesses

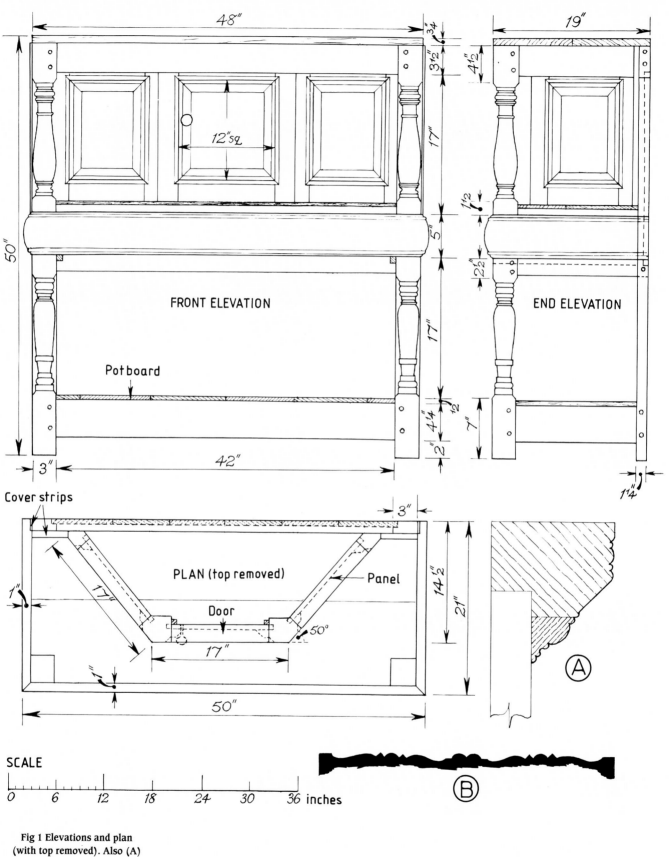

FRONT ELEVATION

END ELEVATION

Potboard

Cover strips

PLAN (top removed)

Panel

Door

SCALE

0   6   12   18   24   30   36 inches

Ⓐ

Ⓑ

Fig 1 Elevations and plan
(with top removed). Also (A)
plan detail of chamfer and
mouldings; (B) suggested
profiles for the cover strips.

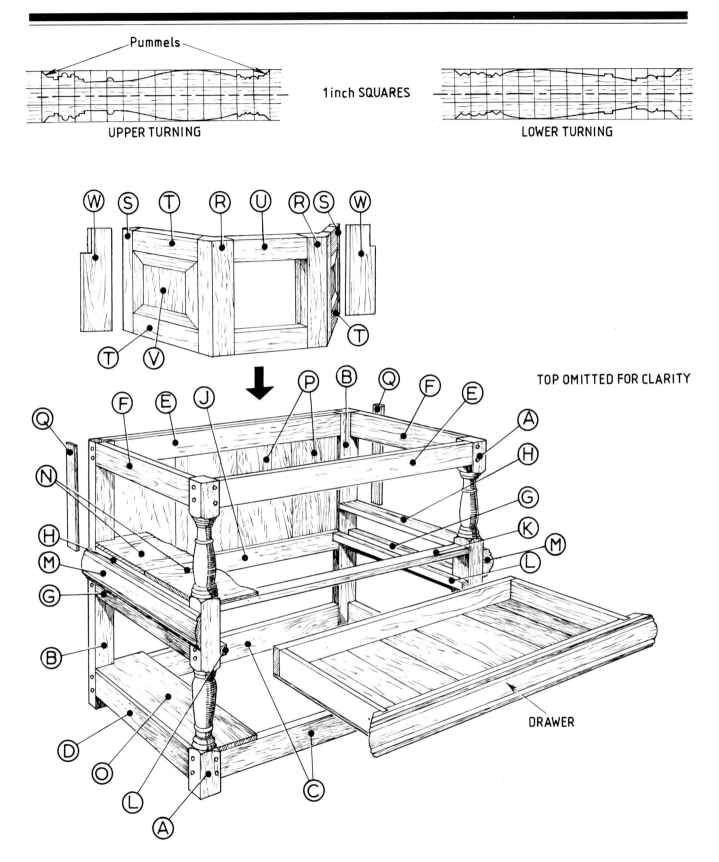

Pummels

1 inch SQUARES

UPPER TURNING

LOWER TURNING

TOP OMITTED FOR CLARITY

DRAWER

Fig 2 Constructional drawing;
plus patterns for upper and
lower turnings on 1 inch
(25mm) grid.

One inch (25mm) squares

Fig 3 (A) repeat pattern on cushion pieces; (B) true section of cushion pieces; (C) door pilaster carving; (D) repeat pattern of ornament on front rails with nail-punched decoration; (E) and (F) inlay patterns for side panel and door panel respectively. Drawn on 1in (25mm) grid.

or 'grounds' for the inlaid patterns can be removed without unduly weakening them, the panels being pinned into rebates as shown in the plan.

The stiles (S) are pinned (or dowelled, if you prefer) to the back rail (E) at the top and pinned (or again, dowelled) to the board (N); this leaves a gap between them and the boards in the back (P) which is hidden by a cover strip (W) pinned on and notched round the rail (F), the fixing being covered by another cover strip (Q), as shown in Fig 2.

Drawer

It was common for drawers of the period to have grooves cut in their sides which engaged with runners fixed to the main frame, thus enabling them to run in and out; in this design, however, the drawer runs on the strips (L).

The drawer sides are housed into a false front and fixed by nailing, the nail heads being covered by the cushion front which, in turn, is pinned on. Nails were also used to fasten the drawer back and the bottom boards, the latter being fixed to the lower edges of the sides and to the back and butted up to the cushion front.

Turnery

The patterns for the upper and lower turnings are shown in Fig 2 and are straightforward enough – note that pummels are turned or chiselled on the squares, depending on your turning skill. There is a reason for this – it is very unlikely that your lathe has a bed long enough to take the full length of each post and consequently you will have to turn it in two parts, joining them by means of pins turned on the ends. The pummels will conveniently hide any small discrepancies.

Decoration and mouldings

The details at Fig 1 (A) and (B) show typical profiles for the stiles, rails and panels, and those on the cover strips respectively. The plain grooves on the end rails were almost certainly worked by a scratch-stock (see Appendix 3), but could be routed with a power router, which could also machine the other mouldings if you don't have a set of moulding planes.

As with the linen chest, the extent to which you embellish the piece is a matter of personal choice, and the patterns are given in Fig 3. The indentations above and below the carved motifs, Fig 3(D), on the top and bottom front rails are decorated with a small punched pattern. The easiest way to do this is with a large 6in (153mm) nail; the pointed end should be cut off square with a hacksaw, and crosswise cuts made on the end, again with the hacksaw. When punched on to the wood the result will be four tiny separate quadrants; you may like to think up other patterns of your own.

Inlays

These are shown in Fig 3 and need to be transferred, full size, to whatever woods you choose; the favourites are holly or poplar for the white parts and bog oak for the black. It is unlikely that you will be able to obtain the latter easily and a good substitute would be sycamore dyed with a black stain. Note that the scale of the diagram is 1in per square.

The wood should be about $^{3}/_{16}$in (5mm) thick, and the larger pieces can be sawn out with a fine fretsaw; you will need to cut the slender stems and scrolls with a sharp craft knife, and it will help if you glue some thin cardboard to the underside to reinforce the wood while you cut it. Use Scotch glue, see Appendix 4, as you will then be able to damp the cardboard and peel it off once the work is done.

Each piece is held down on to the panel and marked around its outline; the recess can then be taken out with a power router or a specially made scratch-stock, depending on its size. Note that the colours of some parts are reversed on one half compared with the other, and for these you will need two pieces, one from each of the woods. Once all the parts have been glued in place and the glue has set completely, go over the whole panel with a scraper, finishing off with a sander.

Finish

A linseed oil or wax finish would be the most appropriate for this particular piece of furniture. Both are described in Appendix 5, Stains, Polishes and Finishes.

Cutting List

	inches			mm		
	L	W	T	L	W	T
2 boards for the top, each	50	10¼	¾	1270	260	19
2 posts (A), each	51	3½	3	1295	89	76
2 back posts (B), each	51	3½	1½	1295	89	38
2 bottom rails (C), each	47	4¾	1½	1193	121	38
2 bottom end rails (D), each	19½	4¾	1½	495	121	38
2 top rails (E), each	47	4	1½	1193	102	38
2 top end rails (F), each	19½	4	1½	495	102	38
2 middle end rails (G), each	19½	3½	1½	495	89	38
2 end rails (H), each	19½	3½	1½	495	89	38
1 back rail (J)	47	3½	1½	1193	89	38
1 front drawer rail (K)	47	3½	1½	1193	89	38
2 drawer runners (L), each	19	1½	1	482	38	25
2 end cushion pieces (M), each	23	6	1½	584	153	38
2 middle stage boards (N), each	50	10¼	½	1270	260	13
Pot boards (O), random widths to cover area (finished size)	48	19½	½	1219	483	13
Back boards (P), random widths to cover area (finished size)	42½	23	½	1079	584	13
2 narrow cover strips (Q), each	21½	1¾	¼	546	45	6.4
2 door muntins (R), each	20	5	3	508	127	76
2 end stiles (S), each	20	4	2	508	102	51
4 panel rails (T), each	14½	3½	2	368	89	51
2 door rails (U), each	14½	3½	2	368	89	51
2 panels (V), each	13½	14	½	343	356	13
2 wide cover strips (W), each	20	5	½	508	127	13
2 door stiles, each	13	2	1½	330	51	38
2 door rails, each	13	2	1½	330	51	38
1 door panel	13	13	½	330	330	13
1 drawer cushion front	52	6	1½	1321	153	38
1 drawer false front	48	5	1	1219	127	25
1 drawer back	48	5	¾	1219	127	19
2 drawer sides, each	17½	5	¾	445	127	19
Random width boards for drawer bottom, to cover area (finished size)	17¼	45	½	438	1143	13

Generous working allowances have been made to lengths and widths; thicknesses are net.

APPENDIX 1: JOINTS AND CABINET WORK

Dovetail joints

These are well-known joints for joining parts together at right angles, and in addition to their strength they have an advantage which may not be apparent at first sight. This is that any tendency of the wood to twist or split is minimized by its being spread over the whole width of the joint – a highly desirable attribute when using solid stuff. The through dovetails shown in Fig 1 (A) are the strongest kind; if a particularly robust joint is required, the spaces between the pins should be equal to the width of the pins themselves, resulting in what are called 'carpenter's dovetails'. The appearance can be improved by making the widest part of the pins equal to, or a trifle larger than, half the thickness of the wood.

A slope of about 82 degrees is considered to be the most suitable for general work, and you will find it worthwhile to make a template from thin plywood or (better still) thin metal sheet. More precisely, the angle required on hardwood can be obtained by drawing a straight line 6in (152mm) long and another line ¾in (19mm) long at right angles to it at one end and joining them. The comparable angle for softwood results from using 6in (152mm) and 1¼in (32mm) lines.

As well as through dovetails there are several other types shown in Fig 1, namely: (B) the single-lap dovetail, used mainly to join drawer sides to the fronts; (C) and (D) double-lap dovetails, the laps being on the tails and the pins respectively. They can be used to join panels together, provided the fact that the lap is visible is not objected to. The mitred dovetail at (E) is employed in high-class work where the joint has to be concealed completely and is consequently sometimes called the 'secret' dovetail. Details are shown in Fig 2(A), (B) and (C).

With the exception of (E), which must be worked by hand, the other joints can be cut with a portable router used in conjunction with one or other of the several dovetailing jigs on the market; lack of space makes it impossible to give explicit details of how to make the joints by hand here, but the following advice should be helpful.

Most woodworkers find it easier to cut the tails first and then mark out the pins from them although it is a matter of personal preference – in the case of (E), however, it is essential to cut the pins first.

If you find it awkward to saw at an angle with the wood held in a vice, try sloping the work so that the sawcuts can be made vertically on one side of each tail and then re-fix the work so that the other side can be sawn in like fashion.

The best way to cut away the bulk of the waste is to use a coping saw, finishing with a sharp chisel. You can use a pencil to transfer the sizes of the tails to the pins but in most circumstances a sharp craft knife or a marking awl will do the job more accurately. You will also find it helpful to use a craft knife to cut small vee-grooves in which you can start the saw cuts and thus make a neater job.

Dealing now with the mitred dovetail at (E) it is obvious that accurate marking out is essential. Both parts have to be exactly the same thickness (x in Fig 2(A)), and the first step is to mark them as shown; the dotted lines indicate the rebates

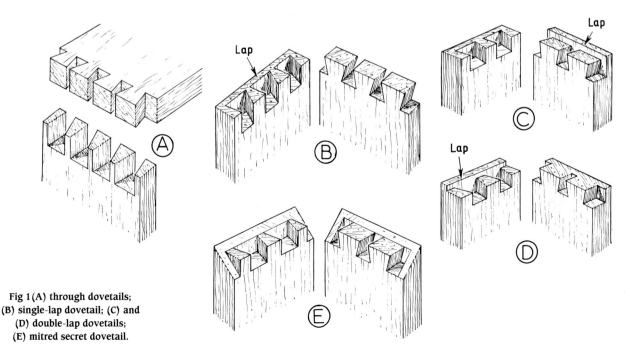

Fig 1 (A) through dovetails; (B) single-lap dovetail; (C) and (D) double-lap dovetails; (E) mitred secret dovetail.

Rebate dotted

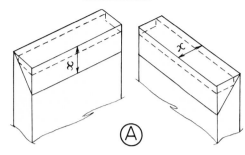

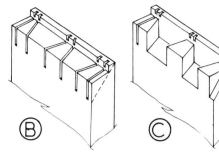

Needle pins

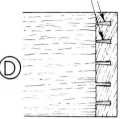

Fig 2(A), (B), and (C) show stages in making the mitred secret dovetail in Fig 1 (E). Finely tapered needle pin dovetails are shown at (D).

which need to be cut away to form a lap on each piece. When you have done this you can mark out the pins, using a template, and start sawing them as at Fig 2(B); it does not matter if you accidentally cut the lap in the process as it is planed off at 45 degrees at a later stage. The waste can then be carefully chiselled away, and the corner mitres sawn as at Fig 2(C).

At this juncture, the piece can be held upright on the end of the matching part and the tails marked out by scribing round them. They can then be sawn and chiselled out in a similar fashion to that employed when cutting the pins. When fitting the joint together, the job can be made easier by paring a sliver away on the front corner of each tail.

Fig 2(D) illustrates what are sometimes called 'needle pin' dovetails, which were a speciality of the best cabinet makers, particularly when making small drawers or caskets.

Edge-to-edge joints

The traditional method when gluing pieces edge to edge was to employ the 'rubbed joint', and it is still one of the best. The pieces must be arranged as shown in Fig 3(A), with their heart sides alternating to lessen the risk of warping.

If the parts are less than 3ft (915mm) long there should be no need to cramp them together as the expulsion of the air between the edges plus the adhesion of the glue should suffice; in the case of longer pieces it is advisable to enlist a helper and also to use two cramps, each one fixed about one-third in from the end. The sketch at (B) shows how long pieces require their meeting edges to be planed slightly hollow to create a gap of about $\frac{1}{16}$in (2mm) in lengths up to 4ft (1220mm), $\frac{1}{8}$in (3mm) in longer lengths. Because the ends of the joint are always the most likely to spring apart, cramping them up until the gap is closed ensures close fitting. Testing the edges of shorter pieces for truth can be done by swivelling one upon the other as at (C), planing them if necessary until the ends rub closely together.

As the joint is a traditional one, it follows that the best adhesive is also traditional – in other words, Scotch glue, which has an immediate tack or 'grab'. It is possible to use polyvinyl acetate (PVA) adhesive if you allow a short time for it to start setting first so that it, too, will grip while the pieces

are being rubbed. Casein-based glues, however, are unsuitable for this job.

If you are using Scotch glue, make sure that the pieces to be joined are warm, as cold wood will chill the glue and spoil the adhesion; if you can arrange for a helper to play a hairdryer along the joint beforehand and while you are working it will help considerably. When you have applied glue to both edges, lose no time in placing the upper piece on to the lower one as shown at (D) and, holding your hands low down on the top piece, rub it backwards and forwards three or four times, finishing with the marks coinciding. Should the glue chill or the joint break, you will need to wash off the glue, let the wood dry and start again.

Once glued, lay the work on its edge resting on a batten propped against a wall as shown at (E) until the glue has set. If you need to joint up three or four pieces, allow the first two to set before rubbing them on to the third, and so on.

Grooved joints

Now that we have machinery to do the hard work accurately and effortlessly, tonguing and grooving or simple grooving is a matter of fitting the appropriate cutters in a portable router or a spindle moulder. The latest technique is 'biscuit jointing' where a power tool called a hand jointer enables you to make crescent-shaped sawcuts in the edge of one board. One half of a biscuit-shaped key (hence the name) of dried compressed wood is glued into the sawcut on one edge and the other half is glued into the matching sawcut on the other edge. The key swells as it absorbs the glue and makes a tight joint.

Fig 3(F) shows two kinds of loose tongue, one being in plywood and the other in hardwood, the important point being that they should always be cross-grained for the greatest strength. Fig 3(G) illustrates a method of joining boards together by means of a simple butt joint, no glue being used. The cleat is screwed across the boards on the underside and round-headed screws driven through slots (not holes) hold it in place but allow the boards to shrink or swell without the whole thing falling apart.

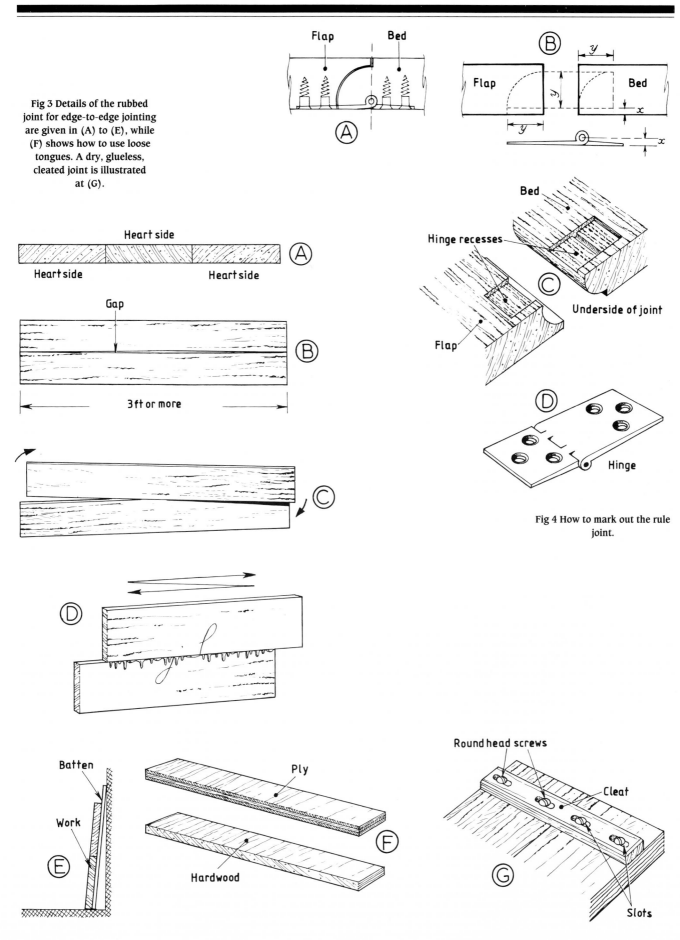

Fig 3 Details of the rubbed joint for edge-to-edge jointing are given in (A) to (E), while (F) shows how to use loose tongues. A dry, glueless, cleated joint is illustrated at (G).

Fig 4 How to mark out the rule joint.

The rule joint

For many years this has been recognized as the best joint for hingeing the flaps of gate-leg tables, card tables and the like, the great advantage being that any pressure applied to the flap is transferred directly to the main bed.

The hinge was in existence long before the arrival of machinery so it can obviously be worked by hand; old-time cabinet makers would have kept a matched pair of moulding planes for the job. Today there are matched pairs of cutters which can be used with a portable router to cut the joint quickly and neatly.

The trickiest part is marking out and working the recesses for the special rule joint hinge (also called a 'table' or 'flap' hinge). Fig 4(A) shows how the centre of the hinge knuckle must be aligned with the vertical lips; at (B) the dimension y determines the radius of the curves, while dimension x governs the depth of the recesses for the hinge leaves; the underside of the joint with the recesses cut out is shown at (C). The hinge is unusual in that the countersinkings on the screw holes are on the opposite side to the knuckle; see Fig 4(D).

Housed joint

This is often employed for fitting shelves, and the kind shown at Fig 5(A) is particularly suitable as it is 'stopped' – that is, the housing is stopped a short distance from the front edge and the shelf is notched out to match, thus effectively hiding all signs of the joint.

Draw-bore tenon

Shown at Fig 5(B), this is one of the oldest joints used for fixing frame rails together and is often found on 16th- and 17th-century furniture. No glue is, or should be, used and the unpredictability of early glues was probably the reason for its origin.

Cut and fit the joint in the usual way, ensuring that the shoulders are a snug fit; then dismantle it and bore a hole right through the mortise as shown. To avoid splitting the walls of the mortise it is a good idea to fill it temporarily with a suitably sized offcut, and also to cramp a piece of waste underneath.

The hole should be about ¼in (6mm) away from the edge, although this dimension could be greater if large pieces are involved.

Once again, fit the tenon into the mortise and push the point of a twist bit through the hole to make a mark on the tenon: withdraw the latter and bore a hole of the same diameter as the first one through it about ¹⁄₁₆in (2mm) in from this mark (see Fig 5(B)). Fit the joint together and force the holes to coincide by knocking in a piece of metal rod of roughly the same diameter. This will pull the tenon inwards and after removing the rod, you can tap in the peg and trim it to length.

On genuinely antique furniture the heads of the pins frequently stand proud of the surrounding surface by ¹⁄₁₆in (2mm) or so; this is often said to have been caused by the wood around the pegs having shrunk and in some cases this may be so, but it is more likely that they were left protruding so that they could be knocked further home if the joint became loose. The pegs were always riven and not sawn as this gave them greater strength, and they were only roughly rounded with a shave or a knife.

Fixing table tops

Three different methods are shown in Fig 6, namely (A) by means of shrinkage plates, (B) pocket screwing and (C) buttoning.

In the earliest furniture, particularly during the 16th century, table tops were often fixed by means of wooden spikes driven into holes bored through the top and the rail beneath. If you are concerned with historical accuracy, bear in mind that these spikes were always riven and shaped like the pegs mentioned above.

The drawing of the shrinkage plate is self-explanatory and the only points to note are (1) that the flange with the two holes should be screwed to the rail with countersunk-head screws and (2) round-headed screws should be used in the slots and should not be tightened down too hard as this would hamper any movement of the top due to shrinking or swelling.

Pocket screwing (Fig 6(B)) merely involves scooping out a pocket in the rail with a gouge and driving a screw into the

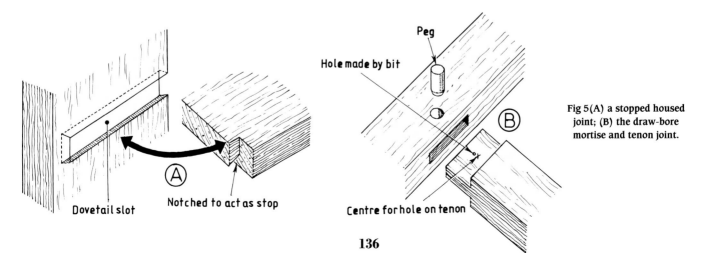

Dovetail slot   Notched to act as stop

Peg

Hole made by bit

Centre for hole on tenon

Fig 5(A) a stopped housed joint; (B) the draw-bore mortise and tenon joint.

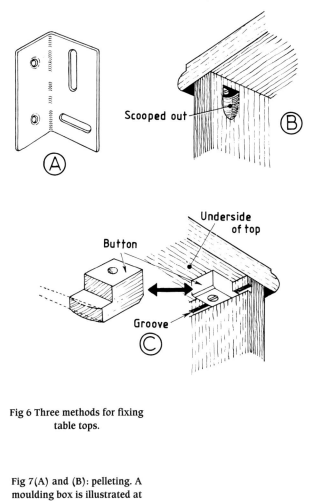

Fig 6 Three methods for fixing table tops.

Fig 7(A) and (B): pelleting. A moulding box is illustrated at (C) and (D).

underside of the top. Note, however, that from about 1850 onwards the pocket was often formed by chiselling out a vee-shape.

Buttoning (Fig 6(C)) is one of the best ways to fix a table top. The buttons can be cut off individually to length from a strip that has had a rebate worked along one edge. The result is a series of small rectangular blocks each of which has a protruding tongue that fits tightly into a groove cut into the frame rail. An added refinement is to taper the tongue to a slight wedge shape as shown by the dotted lines so that the further it enters the groove the tighter it becomes.

Miscellaneous

Figs 7(A) and (B) illustrate two methods of pelleting, a procedure that is used to fill in an unwanted hole or the countersunk recess above a screw head. This can also be done by plugging the hole with a short length of dowel, but this means that the cross-grained end is exposed and soaks up stain and polish to a greater degree than the surrounding grain, which can be unsightly. The plug cutter shown at (A) can be used in a plunge router, or an ordinary power drill mounted in a vertical drill stand. There are several different sizes and the resulting pellets show long grain across their tops which can be matched to the grain of the surrounding area. An alternative method is to turn them on a lathe as shown at (B) and cut them off to length.

The device illustrated at Fig 7(C) is a moulding box and enables you to work mouldings on tapered legs either by hand using a sliding stock as shown, or a portable router in conjunction with support strips as detailed at (D). You really

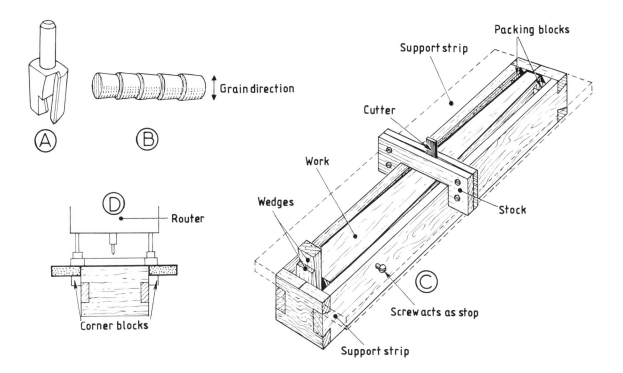

need two such boxes – one for chair legs and another for table legs, which automatically determines their sizes. Chair legs rarely exceed 20in (510mm) in length and 2in (51mm) in thickness, and the corresponding sizes for table legs are 30in (762mm) and 3in (76mm); consequently each box needs to be an inch (25mm) or so larger all round.

The work is fixed in the box by means of wedges and packing blocks, and the latter can also be utilized to bring the leg level with the sides. The box can also be used when forming a taper on a blank: by putting a small wedge under one end of the blank, the upper side can be made to project so that you can plane it off. The dotted lines in (C) indicate strips that can be screwed to the box sides to support the sole plate of a portable router (also shown at D). It may seem old-fashioned to show a wooden stock with a cutter clamped into it but bear in mind that router cutters are very expensive, and a cutter ground and filed to shape at home can be a cheap and effective alternative (the famous French cabinet maker J. A. Roubo gives details of several similar devices in his book *Le menuisier ébéniste*, published in 1772, although some of his designs are more sophisticated than the one shown).

Conventional drawer frame construction

Fig 8 should be fairly self-explanatory but the following points may need further elaboration:

(a) the upper front (or frieze) rail is sufficiently wide for it to be joined to both the corner post and the end rail by what are called 'carcase' dovetails;

(b) the runners are notched round the vertical post and the muntin at the back, but are tenoned into the lower front rail – the dustboard grooves can be used as mortises;

(c) the kicker, which prevents the drawer tilting as it is withdrawn, is mortise and tenoned at each end;

(d) the division is twin tenoned at top and bottom, the tenons being wedged;

(e) the dustboards (not illustrated) are simply thin boards, say ¼in (6mm) thick, which are inserted into the grooves while the framing is being assembled. The term is actually a misnomer as no dust should be able to penetrate a well-made job: their purpose is to prevent the contents of one drawer from jamming against the drawer above.

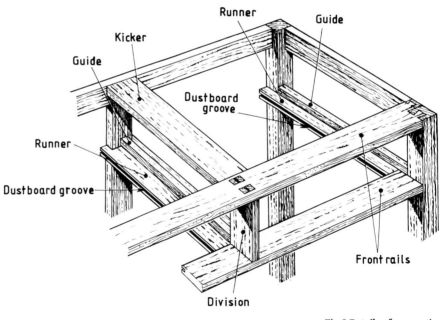

Fig 8 Details of conventional drawer frame construction.

APPENDIX 2: VENEERING

Groundwork

This is the trade term for the base on which a veneer is laid (sometimes called the 'substrate'), and choosing the right one is crucial to success. The ideal is one which absorbs the adhesive evenly over its whole surface, and which does not warp, shrink or twist; the two most obvious candidates are medium density fibre board (MDF), and plywood, provided that the latter is free from knots and that the grain of its outer ply runs at right angles to that of the veneer.

Some solid woods are satisfactory and the best is straight-grained Honduras mahogany; others are birch, American canary whitewood, and obeche. If you are making an authentic reproduction piece it is often necessary to use oak, the grain of which can vary widely in its degree of absorbency, with the result that after a time the pattern of the grain can be traced through modern thin veneers. The best way to overcome this is to veneer on the heart side and use only straight-grained wood, which generally means imported oak such as American, European or Japanese as English oak is frequently wild in the grain.

All groundwork, even MDF, should be counter-veneered (also called 'balancing' or 'compensating' veneering) if it is thinner than ¾in (19mm), and a groundwork made up of strips glued side by side must always be counter-veneered.

The treatment is necessary because the grain of the veneer and the adhesive can exert enough force to bend it out of true over a period of time.

Finally, all groundwork needs to be roughened slightly to provide a key for the adhesive: in the old days when solid wood was employed this was done with a special toothing plane, but today a coarse grade of glasspaper or a rasp is used with equal effect.

Veneering methods

Caul veneering is illustrated in Fig 1 and is used for large flat surfaces, especially if there is a quantity of panels to be done.

Once the veneer has been glued to the groundwork, a sheet of thin plastic film should be laid over it so that any glue squeezed out cannot stick the parts together. The caul needs to be slightly larger all round than the work and is laid on top (one of the cheaper grades of plywood will do). Pressure is applied by cramps tightening down on to the bearers which, in turn, transmit it to the caul as in Fig 1(A). To make the pressure more effective the faces of the bearers are slightly curved, and they should be spaced about 12in (305mm) apart; begin tightening the centre cramps first and work outwards. If you are using Scotch glue the caul should be well

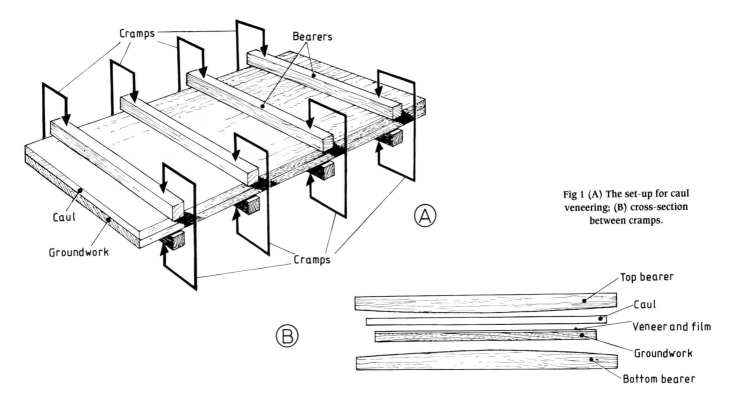

Fig 1 (A) The set-up for caul veneering; (B) cross-section between cramps.

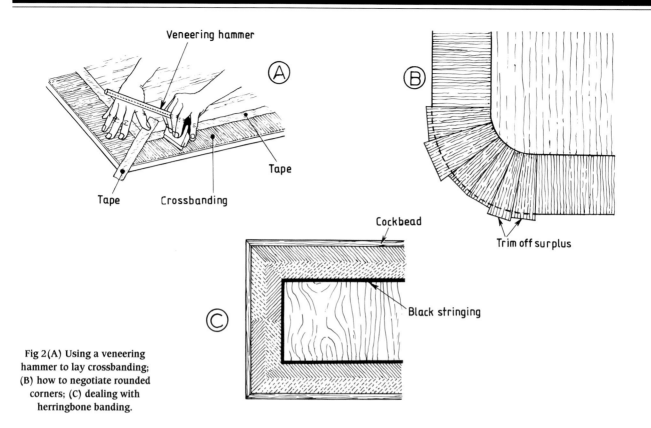

Fig 2(A) Using a veneering hammer to lay crossbanding; (B) how to negotiate rounded corners; (C) dealing with herringbone banding.

heated as if it is cold the glue is likely to chill and become useless.

For small work, particularly crossbanding, you can employ a veneering hammer as in Fig 2(A). This is not used like a normal hammer but is pressed firmly but lightly on the surface and moved in a zigzag motion from the centre outwards.

Matching patterned veneers

Fig 3(A)–(E) shows several of the most frequently employed patterns: (A) halved; (B) quartered; (C) alternating squares; (D) diamond; and (E) reversed diamond matchings.

The method of marking the veneer accurately for a quartered pattern is illustrated in the larger diagram. You will need four consecutive leaves for this, bearing in mind that not only

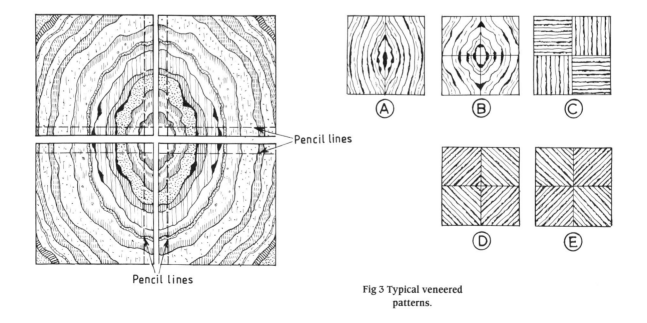

Fig 3 Typical veneered patterns.

must the grain pattern match but so must the reflection of the light from the surface. The pencil lines indicate the overlaps and when the veneer has been laid they should coincide exactly with the centre lines you have already marked on the groundwork.

Cutting the veneer can be done with a craft knife or with a saw if it is strongly figured or very thick. Sticking lengths of gummed brown paper tape over the pieces to be cut will help to stop splintering; it can be removed by wiping over with a damp cloth.

Laying difficult veneers

These include strongly figured 'feathers' and 'curls', which are produced from the junction of a branch from the main trunk, and 'burrs' which are tightly packed buds that have had no chance to develop as a result of undernourishment.

The problem when laying them is that they are 'bumpy' and tend to cockle and obviously need flattening, or 'flatting' as it is called in the trade. You will need to damp the veneer (but only slightly) and then press it between two hot cauls until dry; the cauls can be two sheets of plywood or chipboard which have been heated (behind a hot radiator, for example) for an hour or so. Rosewood, satinwood and teak can also be heated but cannot be damped because of their natural oiliness.

Undoubtedly 'oysters' are the most difficult to season and lay. An oyster is a thin slice, normally about ⅛in (3mm) thick, cut diagonally across a branch so that the result is an oval shape. Although laburnum has long been the favourite other woods such as ash, kingwood, olive and walnut are equally suitable. Freshly cut wood will warp badly; a branch that has been sawn and seasoned for six to twelve months is the best.

The oyster pieces must all be precisely the same thickness when cut, and should be stood on end in a box filled with sawdust; this acts as a buffer between the surrounding atmosphere and the oysters by absorbing excess moisture and thus controlling the seasoning. Even so, many of them will buckle slightly and will need the same treatment as the difficult veneers mentioned above – you can reckon on 50 per cent wastage!

Veneering cylindrical work

This is an old-fashioned technique for veneering cylinders such as those built into pedestals for carrying lamps, vases, ornaments and the like.

The veneer strips are glued to the cylindrical core and then covered with plastic film to prevent any excess glue from sticking where it is not wanted; either string, webbing, or rope (depending on the size of the job) is then wetted and bound around the work, but not too tightly. As the binding dries, it shrinks and exerts considerable pressure; it must be emphasized that the binding must be made from natural fibre such

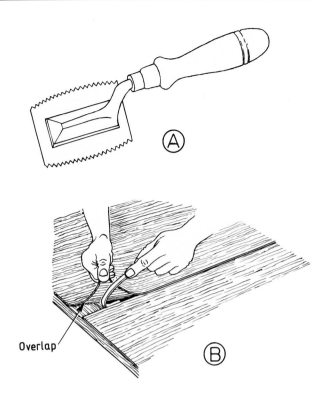

Fig 4(A) a saw specially designed for cutting veneers; (B) ensuring a neat joint.

Overlap

as hessian, sisal, hemp, etc and not plastic. This was a recognized method in the days before impact adhesives began to be used for this kind of work, and a trial run would be advisable.

Laying crossbanding

Fig 2(A) shows this being laid with a veneering hammer – note the paper tape, which should be either proper veneering tape or the gummed brown paper tape obtainable from any stationer. Don't use any of the plastic pressure-sensitive tapes as small splinters of veneer can be broken off when they are removed. The purpose of the tape is, first, to prevent air getting in and creating bubbles and, second, to keep the pieces in place so that the joints do not open while the glue sets.

Dealing with curved corners calls for the treatment shown in Fig 2(B); note how the corner pieces are mitred. Fig 2(C) illustrates herringbone crossbanding laid on a drawer front, and is often found on Queen Anne style furniture; lay the inside strip all round first, and then lay the outside one up to it, making sure the grain pattern matches.

Cutting veneer

There are several ways of doing this and the one you adopt will depend on how thick the veneer is, whether you are cutting with or across the grain, and the sizes of the pieces being worked on.

You can cut the veneer along the grain with the corner of a chisel, but nowadays it is usually done with a craft knife, which is easier to handle. Whichever you choose, support the work on a stout board and cut against a straight edge (preferable a steel one) which should be cramped alongside the line to be followed. It is all too easy for the straight edge to slip unless it is cramped down, and also for the chisel or knife point to follow the grain instead of the line.

Where two edges have to meet, the foolproof way to ensure a faultless joint is to overlap the two pieces by ½in (13mm) or so and arrange that the cutting line falls inside the overlap. Having made the cut, remove the upper waste strip first and then lift up the top sheet and take away the bottom waste; see Fig 4(B).

Working across the grain can only be done by saw – either a fine-toothed back saw, or, better, a proper veneer saw as shown in Fig 4(A). To stop the veneer from splitting or tearing, cramp it between two blocks of straight-edged scrapwood so that the cutting line is tight against them; as the veneer saw has no set to the teeth the projection of the veneer can be very small, which is a distinct advantage.

APPENDIX 3: INLAYS AND BANDINGS

Inlays in solid wood

Once the parts to be inlaid have been drawn they can be cut to shape with a fretsaw; it makes life easier if they are all the same thickness as any standing proud will have to be scraped and glasspapered flush with the others.

Each part is glued down separately into a recess cut out for it. An expansive bit can be used for comparatively small recesses; larger ones can be taken out with a power router and the corners sharpened up with a craft knife if necessary. Be sparing with the adhesive when gluing down; clean off any excess before covering the inlays with a piece of plastic film and weighting them down with a wooden block on which you can put some heavy tools or books.

Making fans and spandrels

The stages in making a fan are illustrated in Fig 1 (A), (B), and (C). Once you have sawn or cut the five tapered pieces slightly oversize to allow for trimming at both ends, they need to be shaded; do this by dipping the edges into hot sand until the correct shade results. The sand can be heated in something like a large old saucepan placed on a gas ring or hotplate; a 1in (25mm) depth of sand should suffice.

Next, assemble by sticking gummed brown paper tape or proper veneering tape on the back, and then mark the outlines to be cut on the face. The cutting can be done with a craft knife or a veneer saw, or a combination of both; alternatively you could cramp the assembly on to a block of waste wood and chop round the outlines with chisels or gouges until the finished fan is as shown in Fig 1 (C).

The spandrel at (D) can be made in similar fashion but there is the added complication of the curved stringing. This can be bent by soaking it in hot water for a few minutes and then working it backwards and forwards across a suitably sized rounded object such as a metal can.

If you prefer, you can buy both fans and spandrels ready made from World of Wood (see Suppliers' List on page 158).

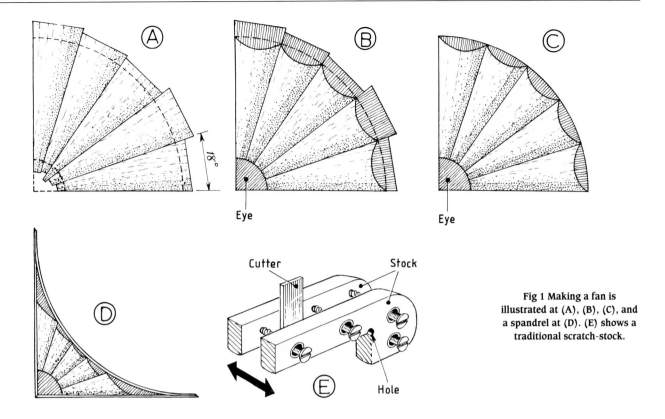

Fig 1 Making a fan is illustrated at (A), (B), (C), and a spandrel at (D). (E) shows a traditional scratch-stock.

Stringings, lines and bandings

There is a difference between the first two, although the names are often used indiscriminately. A line is a piece of veneer that rarely exceeds ¼in (6mm) in width, while a stringing is a thin piece of veneer which is square in section so that a 1mm thick veneer yields a 1mm square line and so on. World of Wood list four sizes: 1mm; ¹⁄₁₆in (2mm); ⅛in (3mm); and ¼in (6mm)

Bandings can be made from one kind of wood as in crossbanding, or from several contrasting woods glued together in such a way as to present attractive patterns such as the typical bandings shown in Fig 2. Again, World of Wood have a wide range of patterns ready made-up.

If you need to make your own, it is quite straightforward and the procedure is shown in Fig 2. Diagram (C) shows the finished banding, and the first step in making it is to glue strips of wood together side by side as at (A). Note how the grain is arranged to display a chevron pattern, and that the work is mounted on a wooden block with a piece of plastic film interposed so that any excess glue does not stick the whole thing together. Both the upper and lower faces must be flush, and once the adhesive has set the work can be removed and the outer veneers glued on as at (B). Finally, once this glue has set, the banding (C) can be sawn off rather like a slice from a loaf of bread.

Herringbone bandings can be made in a similar fashion as illustrated at (AA), (BB) and (CC). Whichever you make up always saw the bandings slightly thicker than the finished size to allow for glasspapering.

Scratch-stock

Although this has been used for centuries to work mouldings it is still a desirable piece of equipment today and is indispensable for some jobs such as the reeding on posts that are both turned and shaped.

Fig 1(E) shows a typical example; the stock can be made from any convenient piece of hardwood and a handy size is 8in (203mm) long by 2½in (64mm) deep by 1¼in (32mm) thick. The cutter can be hacksawn to the required shape and profile (the reverse of the moulding) from a piece of scraper steel; this is obtainable from any good woodworking supplier.

The hole shown allows sawdust to escape instead of clogging up and causing the stock to run out of true; note that the bearing surfaces are slightly rounded so that the stock will run smoothly – a touch of candle wax helps too. The right-angled shape illustrated is the most usual but it is by no means the only one as the idea can be adapted for special work such as the posts mentioned above and for cutting the grooves for stringings and lines.

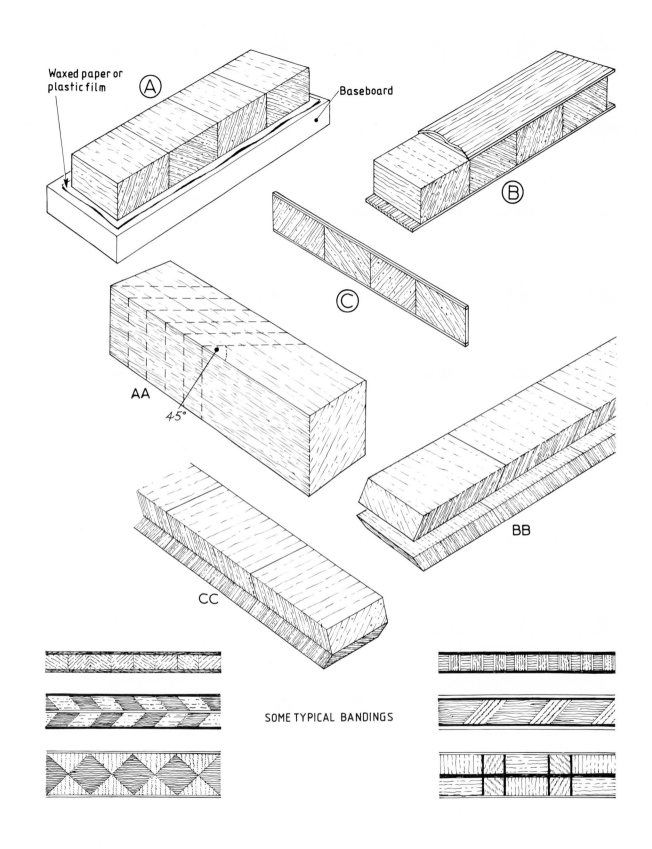

Waxed paper or plastic film

Ⓐ

Baseboard

Ⓑ

Ⓒ

AA

45°

BB

CC

SOME TYPICAL BANDINGS

Fig 2 How to build up and cut
   your own bandings.

Laying stringings, lines and bandings

The recesses or grooves can be made with a scratch-stock fitted with a cutter having the appropriate profile; while this is easy enough to run along the grain it can be difficult to cut across the grain without the edges splintering. To prevent this, cut the edges first with a chisel or a craft knife and then remove the centre with the scratch-stock. For those who have a lot of this kind of work to do there are proprietary devices available, but they are expensive.

The above presupposes that the recesses or grooves are too small or inaccessible to be routed out with a power router (if you have one) as this does the job best of all.

Depending on the width, you can use a veneer hammer to lay wide bandings, or the pene of an ordinary hammer for narrow stringings. In both cases, do not make the recess or groove too deep as the banding or stringing should stand very slightly proud of the surface to ensure that the hammer presses it down even when it is fully home. If you are using Scotch glue it will shrink as it dries out and take the banding with it, otherwise it can be scraped and glasspapered flush.

To avoid bruising the banding or stringing, you can protect it by covering it first with plastic film and then rubbing down on a strip of scrap veneer placed over this – the film prevents any surplus glue from sticking to the scrap veneer.

When laying stringing or banding around a curve, the arrangement illustrated in Fig 3 should be employed and left in place until the glue has set.

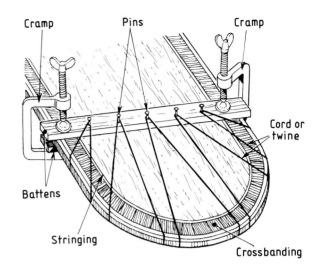

Fig 3 An easy and effective way to hold stringing or banding around a curve while the glue sets.

APPENDIX 4: ADHESIVES

Scotch glue

Also called 'animal' or 'hide' glue, this is one of the oldest of adhesives. It has been used since the beginning of the 17th century – a ruling of the Committee of the Court of Aldermen in 1632 decided that joiners were permitted to make 'all tables of wainscote, walnutt, or other stuffe, glued with frames, mortesses, and tenants'. Before 1600 or thereabouts the glue was difficult to obtain and keep from going mouldy, also it was unreliable in its bonding abilities; hence the practice of using dry mortise and tenon joints with the tenons pinned so that any kind of glue was unnecessary.

It is normally sold in pearl or powder form although at one time it was also supplied in sheets or 'cakes' that had to be broken into small pieces. Whichever kind you buy needs to be soaked overnight, preferably in a glass jar (unless you have a proper double glue pot in which case you can use the inner pot). One of the best receptacles is an ovenproof jug which can cope with both the soaking and the heating processes. The glue has an indefinite shelf life if it is kept dry and cool; it is best to make up a new supply every day.

By morning the glue will have coalesced into a thick mass which you will have to stir with a piece of stick as you heat it. Stand the jug on a couple of small wooden blocks in the bottom of a saucepan half-filled with cold water; the blocks allow the water to circulate around the bottom of the jug where the glue is usually thickest.

The optimum working temperature is about 160°F (71°C). This is about the same as for many domestic hot water systems, so water from the hot tap can be used for diluting the glue or topping up the saucepan. Check the consistency from time to time by lifting the stick and letting the glue run back into the jug; it should run in a continuous stream with no lumps and without breaking into separate drops – a consistency roughly akin to single dairy cream. The glue must never be allowed to boil as this weakens it.

All the parts which are to be glued must be warmed as cold surfaces chill the glue and render it useless; you can stand the parts at a safe distance from an electric or gas fire or around the workshop stove, and it helps considerably if a helper plays a hairdryer on the work as it progresses. You need to work quickly, so all ancillary equipment must be kept handy: all cramps should be opened to the requisite amount, cramping blocks should be ready for insertion, and a measuring and testing rod kept nearby.

One of the great advantages of Scotch glue is that it has a good initial 'tack' (which means that it grips instantly) but still allows the parts to be moved relative to one another which is ideal for rub-jointing and hammer veneering. Another advantage is that a glued-up joint can easily be disassembled by applying steam to it, or wrapping it in a cloth which has been soaked in hot water and wrung out; a 50/50 mixture of vinegar and cold water will also do the job.

Polyvinyl acetate (PVA) adhesive

This is now the most widely used woodworking adhesive as it is easy to store and trouble-free in use. The basic ingredients are derived from petroleum compounds and acetylene gas, combined to yield a white emulsion of PVA globules suspended in water; consequently it is possible to dilute the adhesive with water as we shall see when we describe how to lay leather linings on page 153.

This affinity with water affects the efficacy of the adhesive in conditions of high and low humidity – it will not bond wood with a moisture content higher than 12 per cent or lower than 4 per cent – in the latter case the wood absorbs the water from the adhesive before the joint can be assembled. Temperature is critical too; below 45°F (7°C) the adhesive becomes grainy and crumbles, thus failing to give a workable glue line; while above 100°F (37°C) it skins over so quickly that there's little opportunity to assemble the parts accurately.

The adhesive has virtually no initial tack and is therefore unsuitable for rubbed joints or hammer veneering unless you allow ten minutes or so for some of the water to evaporate; the actual time has to be judged according to prevailing conditions of temperature and humidity. Both surfaces to be joined should receive a thin coating – the thinner the better when gluing veneer as too much adhesive will contain an excess of water which could cause the veneer to warp.

In normal circumstances the work should be kept cramped up for about six hours, although final setting continues for a day or so. Wipe away any surplus adhesive with a damp cloth as soon as possible.

The adhesive is generally marketed in a squeezy bottle with a handy nozzle for application; its shelf life is a year or two if stored at room temperature with an airtight nozzle. A disadvantage is that the adhesive has a slight tendency to 'creep' under a heavy load or continuous stress; this can be beneficial, however, as it can help to accommodate any movement of the wood due to swelling or shrinkage.

Adhesives for bonding metal to wood

The metal involved is usually brass sheet in the form of decorative shapes or inlaid lines, and the easiest and most effective method is to use an epoxy resin such as Araldite or one of the Bostiks; full instructions are given in the manufacturers' leaflets.

For those who want historical authenticity, there are alternatives. One is to insert a flake of shellac between the brass and the wood and heat up the brass with a soldering iron set at a low heat. This will melt the shellac, and if the brass is pressed down a good bond should result.

Another alternative is to use freshly made Scotch glue with a little plaster of Paris mixed into it; it helps considerably if the back of the brass is scored to form a key and then rubbed with a clove of garlic, which acts as a mordant.

APPENDIX 5: STAINS, POLISHES AND FINISHES

Oil finishes have been employed since the early 16th century until the present day with very little change in their ingredients, while others such as the shellac finish, the wax finish, French polish and the various varnishes have each had their own periods of popularity.

The oil finish

Originally linseed oil on its own was used for this. The raw oil is preferable to the boiled kind which tends to soften if it is subject to warmth – even the natural heat of the fingers – and it never seems to harden off as well as the raw oil.

Whichever oil you use it is worthwhile keeping it warm while you use it by immersing the container in a bowl of hot water. If you want to make applying it even easier, first heat it gently for a quarter of an hour or so, making sure it does not boil; then take if off the heat and stir in one-eighth by volume of pure turpentine if you have it, or failing this, the same quantity of best-quality turpentine substitute (also called white spirit). To speed drying you could add 1 teaspoonful of terebene driers to each half-pint (0.28 litres).

The secret of applying the oil is not to flood the wood but to scrub it into the grain with a shoe brush and then wrap a piece of thick cloth such as flannel or felt around an ordinary housebrick or something similar in size and weight and rub the oil into the surface, using plenty of elbow grease. The wood will always take more oil, unless you have previously filled the grain with a grain filler, and the process needs to be repeated daily over a couple of weeks, and then once or twice a year.

This yields a beautifully glowing surface which will not crack, blister or show marks; it is also a sympathetic finish in the sense that most marks which may appear can be rubbed away with a trace of oil on a soft, lint-free cloth. The finish does have the disadvantage of darkening in colour over the years, although this is a desirable quality to many people.

Teak is a notoriously greasy timber for which the oil finish is particularly suitable. You will need to wipe the surface first with plenty of turpentine substitute to remove as much of the natural oil as possible, and then apply the oil as soon as the turps has evaporated. If you want to make daily applications, try a mixture based on half a pint (0.28 litres) of the linseed oil plus one-tenth by volume of turpentine (or turps substitute) and four or five drops of terebene driers.

Water stains

To get a special colour you can either (a) stain the wood or (b) colour the oil itself, as recommended by Thomas Sheraton. In the case of (a) proprietary water stains can be used, the disadvantage being that they tend to raise the grain and in glasspapering the surface to get rid of this, it is all too likely that some of the stain will be papered away, resulting in a patchwork of different shades. To avoid this, before you apply the stain wipe over the wood with a rag dipped in cold water; allow it to dry thoroughly and glasspaper it with a fine grade of paper to get rid of any fibres.

There are several other water stains you can make for yourself, as follows.

Copperas (ferrous sulphate). Dissolving a teaspoonful of the crystals to a pint (0.56 litres) of water gives a medium blue stain which can be diluted or concentrated as required. A pale-blue shade will kill the redness of mahogany so that it resembles walnut; it will also turn sycamore grey, thus producing harewood.

Bichromate of potash crystals. Dissolve the crystals in water until the solution is saturated and use this as a concentrated stock solution from which you can draw and dilute as required. The solution is a rich orange colour, but when used on mahogany it produces a deep cold brown, and a greenish-brown tint on oak. It will not affect timbers which do not contain tannic acid (such as pine and whitewoods) unless they are first primed with tannic or pyrogallic acid. The stain is 'fugitive' – that is, it will fade in strong sunlight. Wear protective gloves as the crystals are poisonous and can harm the skin.

Potassium permanganate crystals. These dissolve easily in water and produce a rich purple-coloured stain which, when applied to a light-coloured wood, gives a walnut colour. Unfortunately it is very fugitive and cannot be recommended although it is often quoted in books and magazines.

John Evelyn in his book *Sylva* (1664) refers to beech being washed over with a decoction made of the green husks of walnuts in order to make it resemble walnut. Apparently the stain was made by soaking the green husks in rainwater for several days and then adding bicarbonate of soda at the rate of one teaspoonful per gallon (4.5 litres) to act as a binder. The liquid was then heated slowly and kept simmering (but not boiling) for a couple of days, then allowed to cool before being strained into bottles and thereafter kept in a dark place.

Another ancient stain was made by leaving a handful of iron nails to steep in a quart (1.13 litres) of ordinary vinegar for a week or so. The strength of the solution was controlled by the number of nails and the time allowed for steeping; at its strongest it gave oak a flat, dead black colour.

The coloured oil referred to in (b) above is a recipe to use on mahogany using alkanet root and dragon's blood as the two colouring agents. Alkanet is the old name for the familiar anchusa flowering plant that is grown in many gardens;

dragon's blood is a brilliant red powder made from a gum exuded from the East Indian dragon tree and widely stocked by polish suppliers.

Here is the recipe as it appears in Thomas Sheraton's *Cabinet Dictionary* (1803):

Alkanet was much in use amongst cabinet-makers, for making red oil; the best composition for which, as far as I know, is as follows: take a quart [1.13 litres] of good linseed oil, to which put a quarter of a pound [113 grams] of alkanet root, as much opened with the hand as possible, that the bark of the root which tinges the oil may fly off; to this put an ounce [28 grams] of dragon's blood, and another of rose pink, finely pounded in a mortar; set the whole within a moderate heat for twelve hours at least, or better if a day and a night. Then strain it through a flannel into a bottle for use. This staining oil is not applicable to every sort of mahogany … [mahogany that is] close grained and hard and wants briskness of colour, the above oil will help it much. All hard mahogany of a bad colour should be oiled with it, and should stand unpolished a time, proportioned to its quality and texture of grain; if it is to be laid on hard wood to be polished off immediately, it is of little use; but if it stand a few days after, the oil penetrates the grain and hardens on the surface, and consequently will bear a better polish, and look brighter in colour.

There is another recipe that uses alkanet root to colour linseed oil, and this involves bruising about 4oz (113g) of alkanet roots with a hammer; it helps if they are cut into short strips first. They are then steeped for two or three days in a pint (0.56 litres) of raw linseed oil to which a tablespoonful of turpentine substitute has been added, keeping the concoction in a warm place (the airing cupboard should be ideal) and stirring it occasionally. It should then be thoroughly strained and bottled, diluting it with more oil if necessary. Unfortunately alkanet root does not appear to be a commercial product and you will have to sacrifice a plant from the garden!

All of the above stains can be used equally successfully with a shellac finish or a wax finish.

The shellac finish (*also known as 'spirit varnish'*)

Natural shellac, before it is processed, consists of the hardened secretions of lac insects which are found in abundance on the branches and twigs of trees in India and Thailand; it began to be imported into Europe from about 1650, when trade was opened up with the East.

The raw shellac has to be melted, purified, and converted into small flakes or buttons (the latter form gives us 'button polish'); it is sometimes bleached as well. It forms the basis of the well-known French polish which will be described later; here we are concerned with brushing on shellac to create the traditional finish used during the 18th century. Obviously the shellac has to be dissolved to form a solution, and the liquid used is best quality industrial alcohol or, for home woodworkers, methylated spirit.

You can make up your own varnish by dissolving orange shellac flakes in methylated spirit at the rate of 2lb (0.9kg) of flakes to 1 gallon (4.5 litres); this is known in the trade as a '2lb cut'. The solution has a short shelf life and should be made up as and when needed. The bottle must be kept tightly sealed with a cork or a metal cap; it can be stirred but must never be shaken because this will create air bubbles.

Alternatively, you can use a proprietary brushing French polish, which is strongly recommended as it contains an additive to help it spread evenly – one great disadvantage of the home-made solution is that it is difficult to apply evenly.

In all cases the best brush to use is a polisher's mop; pour the polish into something like a pudding basin and press the brush against the side to get rid of any excess without creating air bubbles. It helps if the basin can stand in warm water as the polish spreads best if its temperature is about 70°F (22°C); this should also be the temperature of the workshop, and the air must be dry as too much humidity will cause the polish to 'bloom' and appear as a milky white film. It is also essential to keep dust off the surface, so avoid wearing woolly cardigans or pullovers.

Each coat takes an hour or so to dry, when another one can be applied; six coats or more will give a glowing lustrous finish. Unfortunately the surface can easily be marked by water, heat or chemicals and it's a good idea to allow the last coat to dry overnight and then apply a coat of best-quality wax polish as this will confer some extra protection.

Wax polishes

These have been used since the middle of the 16th century when fireplaces built into the walls of houses replaced the central hearths which allowed smoke to drift about and soil everything before finding its way out through holes or louvres in the roof; this meant that woodwork had to be repainted every spring (the origin of spring cleaning) – polishing furniture with oils or waxes made this a thing of the past.

The linseed oil finish which has already been dealt with (walnut oil was also used occasionally in a similar fashion) was looked upon primarily as a preservative; the fact that it also darkened the colour of the wood was unfortunate but not important.

Wax polishes do not colour the surface unduly unless required to do so; they do, however, impart a beautiful lustre and patina which improve with regular applications over the years. Because of these qualities and the comparative ease with which they can be applied, they have remained popular until the present day.

Present-day practice is to brush on two coats of clear shellac and allow them to dry before applying the wax polish as this prevents any dust from being rubbed into the grain of the wood; it does, however, mean that you will not get such a deep lustre. In the 17th century the omission of the sealing coats of shellac had another result, which is that the antiqued finish so admired by many people today was produced accidentally by generations of servants polishing the furniture without removing the dust first, resulting in a darker colour being produced around the edges of any panels and in the deeper parts of any carving.

There are many good proprietary waxes available, including some which will stain the wood at the same time as they polish it; avoid any silicone or quick-drying wax polishes; although they have their uses they are not to be recommended for our type of work. If you prefer to make your own polish, here are three useful recipes.

Basic polish. Shred yellow or brown beeswax (a potato peeler or a nutmeg grater is handy for this) and dissolve it in pure turpentine or good quality turpentine substitute. Standing the container in a saucepan of hot water will speed things up; stir the polish until it has the consistency of thin cream.

Light coloured polish. As above but use bleached beeswax.

White coloured polish. Mix in a white powder colour to the light coloured polish – this polish will leave minute traces of a white deposit in the grain of the wood.

Apply all wax polishes with a shoe brush or a lint-free cloth – the brush is particularly useful for carvings, mouldings, and turnings – and rub off any excess with a coarse cloth or a piece of canvas. Allow the polish a couple of hours to dry and repeat the process; after several hours the surface can be buffed up with a soft lint-free cloth or a polishing bonnet fitted to a power drill.

French polishing

This kind of finish arrived from France in the 1820s and immediately became popular – some would say too popular, as the Victorians often had 18th-century furniture stripped and refinished with French polish.

If you are not concerned with authenticity there are several proprietary finishes such as Furniglas, Duraxalin, Wincote and others that give the appearance of French polish without the need for special skills, and they are also more resistant than traditional French polish to spills and other domestic hazards. They should be applied in accordance with the manufacturer's instructions because methods vary according to the differences in formulation.

French polishing, like upholstery or wood carving, is a skilled trade on its own, and while the information given should enable you to make a reasonably good job, only practice will produce results of consistently high quality.

Probably no other finish gives such a hard brilliant shine combined with a deep lustre that shows wood off to its best advantage, but unfortunately it is easily marked by water, heat or spirits; indeed spilt alcohol dissolves it.

Types of French polish

The polish consists of shellac dissolved in industrial alcohol, which is only available to the trade. From our point of view methylated spirit is virtually the same thing but contains additives to make it unpalatable. You could make your own polish by dissolving shellac in methylated spirit, but as there is such a wide range of colours and grades offered by polish suppliers at reasonable prices, it is hardly worth the bother. The standard types are given below; most of them are available in either hard or soft quality.

Button polish. So-called because it is made from shellac shaped like translucent buttons. It is best used for warm golden brown shades; when applied over a dark stain, it will tend to give a muddy colour.

Garnet polish. A dark polish and the one most frequently used for antiques.

French polish. A medium brown colour.

White polish. A light-coloured, almost clear polish made from bleached shellac.

Transparent white polish. This is colourless and very hard, and is made from bleached and de-waxed shellac.

Black polish. Used for jet black and ebonized finishes.

Brush polish. This contains an additive to slow down the drying time, thus making the polish flow on more easily. Particularly useful for turned work.

Equipment

You can store the polish in plastic or glass bottles, labelling each with its contents. Screw-on caps should be pierced with two holes per cap (one hole allows the polish to be shaken out drop by drop and the other enables replacement air to enter). You will also need several screw-top jars – the kind used for instant coffee are ideal – for storing fads and rubbers (see below), using separate jars for each.

A fad is a piece of special wadding sold by polish suppliers which you use to apply and build up the polish; do not attempt to use ordinary cotton wool as it is unsuitable for this purpose.

To prepare the fad, take a piece of wadding about 10in (250mm) square and soak it in polish; allow it to dry, soften it with methylated spirit and wring it out – this will stop loose threads from sticking to the work. Fig 1 shows the stages in folding the wadding to make a fad. It is rather complicated so try a few practice runs first, damping the wadding with water instead of polish. Shape the fad to fit your hand; (G) shows the way to hold it in your fingers.

The rubber is employed to give a final finish to the surface once it has been built up by the fad; the rubber itself is simply a fad with a piece of cloth folded over it. You must choose the right kind of cloth which should ideally be linen but could be cotton; man-made textiles are not absorbent enough.

While you are fadding the surface you will need a small quantity, say about half an eggcupful, of either raw linseed oil or preferably white oil (sometimes called 'mineral oil' or 'white mineral oil'), which does not thicken so easily and is less greasy than linseed.

Fadding

Arrange the work against the light so that you can see the marks where the fad has been. As far as possible make the strokes towards and away from your body, since if you move your arm from side to side the strokes will be in the shape of an arc, which is undesirable. To charge the fad, open the folds and drop in enough polish to make it fairly wet; then press it on to a piece of paper or cardboard to spread the polish evenly.

Start by working backwards and forwards and along the grain, pressing down firmly to force the polish into the pores all over the surface. Repeat the process two or three times until there is a thin film all over, recharging the fad when necessary; Fig 2(A) shows what the path of the fad should be during this stage. Allow the film to dry and then flatten it by papering it very lightly with the finest grade of glasspaper held in the fingers.

Recharge the fad, but flick a few drops of oil on the surface of the work before using it to spread the oil all over the area, pressing down very lightly and moving in arcs. An oily smear will indicate the path of the fad, the purpose being to lubricate its passage over the polish. Too much oil will cause the fad to skid, so wipe the surplus off with a clean rag and go over the surface again until the oil is spread evenly.

With the fad charged with polish, work it over the surface as shown at Fig 2(B) by making small circles around the edges and filling in with large loops. The fad will move easily at first because the oil acts as a lubricant but it will gradually stiffen with use, so apply plenty of pressure and recharge it from time to time. You will see bright patches appearing as the polish takes off the oil, and the pores should appear well filled with polish. If ridges form round the path of the fad (they are called 'whips' and are caused by excess polish oozing out) try to rub them down immediately. If this is unsuccessful, allow the polish to dry thoroughly and rub them down with fine glasspaper lubricated with a few spots of oil; then wipe away the dust and oil and go over the surface once again with the fad. Next change its path to the long figures-of-eight shown at (C), gradually converting them to the straight strokes shown at (D).

Use a rubber next instead of the fad, charging it by unwrapping the outer folds and dripping in just enough polish so that when you pinch the point it just oozes through. Move the rubber in long parallel strokes with the grain as illustrated in (E), gliding the rubber on and off at the ends of the strokes – dabbing it on to the surface will ruin it. The surface should be bright and quite free from oil and you should leave it for 24

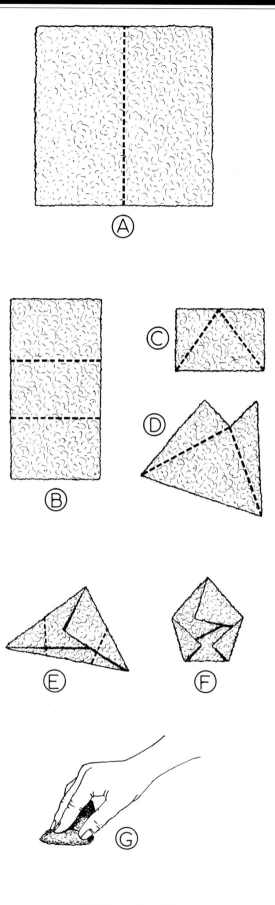

Fig 1 Preparing a fad.

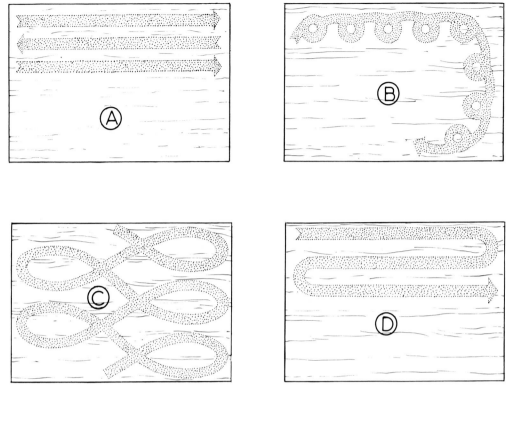

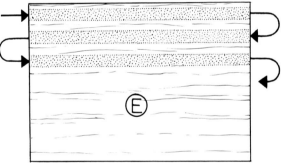

Fig 2 Strokes and movements
of the fad and the rubber used
in French polishing.

hours to harden. At this juncture any small holes or cracks can be filled with a proprietary shellac filler stick, and when this has been done you can move on to 'bodying up'.

Flick a few drops of oil on to the surface of the work and glide on your rubber which should be charged with polish to begin this stage. Fig 3(A) shows the strokes which you should employ to distribute the oil evenly over the surface by making small figures-of-eight around the edges with larger ones in the centre. Then gradually change to the long figures-of-eight shown at (B), charging the rubber when necessary –

normally about three times. Change slowly to the movement shown at (C), when the surface should be smooth and glossy; any oil remaining on it can be wiped off with a clean rag moistened with methylated spirit. This may dull the surface slightly but this will be taken care of in the next stage.

You will need to make up a separate rubber for the next step, which is the finishing. This rubber must be kept exclusively for this particular job. You will need to make a 50/50 mixture of polish and methylated spirit for charging the rubber.

Flick a few drops of oil on the surface and spread it evenly with the charged rubber. Use a light even pressure, moving it in circles with an occasional straight stroke along the grain until the rubber is dry. The surface should then be covered with a thin, delicate film of oil.

Carry on immediately by 'spiriting off', which is the final stage. Another rubber is required for this and it too must be kept for this job and no other. To charge it, apply a few drops of methylated spirit to the fad; test for the correct amount of spirit by touching the fad to your lips – it should not be wet, but cold and sharp. Wrap the fad in its cloth to make a rubber, and glide it on the surface, moving it rapidly with firm pressure in long figures-of-eight and circles. This will remove all traces of oil and also burnish the surface so that it looks lustrous and glass-like. By dipping the face of the rubber into Vienna chalk and rubbing the surface with long strokes you will improve the finish even more.

Varnishes

Until the advent of synthetic resins, these consisted of either an oil or a spirit base in which natural resins and gums were dissolved. These 'natural' varnishes have been supplanted almost exclusively by polyester and polyurethane lacquers in Britain. In the USA, Behlen's polish suppliers offer a range of natural resin varnishes available from Garrett Wade (see Suppliers' List).

Full instructions are given on the cans of synthetic lacquers, which are very straightforward to apply.

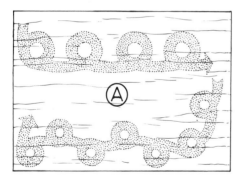

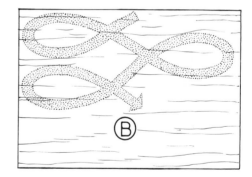

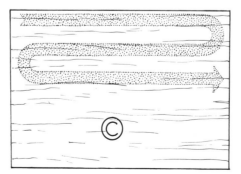

Fig 3 Oiling strokes using a rubber, continued.

APPENDIX 6: LEATHER LINING AND UPHOLSTERY

Leather 'skivers'

This is the name given to the sheepskins which are used to line writing-table tops, bureaux flaps and the like. Because they are animal products their size is rarely larger than 40in by 24in (1016mm by 610mm); if a larger piece is required the supplier can join two smaller ones together.

A skiver can be supplied in any one of nine colours – beige, black, blue, bottle green, brown, maroon, old gold, olive green or red – and have its edges blind-tooled. A gilt tooling can be added as well if you wish and a wide range of patterns is available. Give the exact dimensions of the piece you need; the supplier will always make an extra allowance for trimming.

Laying leather

To stick down leather you can use either a wallpaper cold water paste made slightly thicker than usual, or a PVA woodworking adhesive diluted in the proportion of four parts adhesive to one of water.

Start by cutting one long edge of the leather to fit, and then apply the adhesive all over the recess using a brush to spread it evenly. Next, place this long edge tight up against the margin and rub it down from the centre outwards with a soft cloth; then continue rubbing down in the sequence shown by the arrows in Fig 1. The surface should be free of air bubbles and wrinkles and should feel taut but not stretched.

The leather will stretch a little anyway, and you will have to trim it to fit the recess neatly. Feel for the edge and run your fingernail along it to make a crease and then cut along this with a sharp craft knife (Fig 2). Ease the waste away as you go and keep the blade at a slight angle and twisted a little so that it tends to cut the wood rather than the leather. By holding the knife at this slight angle the edge of the leather will be bevelled so that the unstained side will not show.

To negotiate a corner, hold the waste out of the way and make a cut from the opposite direction to meet the first one. Finally run your thumbnail all round the edges to press them home, and then leave the work to dry for half an hour; on your return check to see if any bubbles or wrinkles have developed as you will need to rub them out. If the leather is likely to be subjected to continual creasing (as is the case with some writing slopes), a strip of linen can be glued on the underside with the same adhesive to act as a reinforcement.

Loose seat – traditional style

The frame for this is best made in beech, which is easily obtainable and holds tacks well. Construction is straightforward as the frame utilizes simple halved joints which are nailed and glued together. If you have a staple gun suitable for upholstery work you can use it instead of a hammer and tacks.

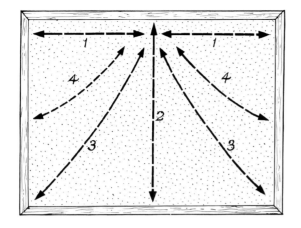

Fig 1 Smoothing down the leather to exclude air bubbles and wrinkles.

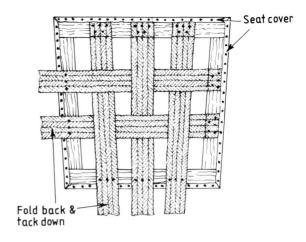

Fig 3 Arrangement of webs on a typical loose seat.

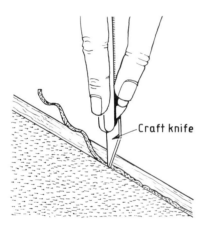

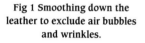

Fig 2 Trimming the edges.

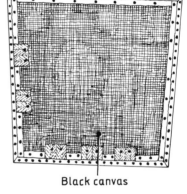

Fig 4 Tacking down the webs.

To fully upholster a seat in the traditional manner, tack on the webs as shown in Fig 3, starting with the front-to-back webs and finishing with the side ones. Note that the ends of half of the webs are left loose, to be tacked down later over the hessian covering (see Fig 4).

Now tack on a piece of hessian with ⅜in (10mm) or ½in (13mm) improved tacks, spacing them about ¾in (19mm) apart and keeping the weave of the hessian parallel to the seat frame as far as possible. The best method is to turn the edge of the hessian over by about ¾in (19mm) and start with one tack at the centre of the front rail; stretch the hessian taut and insert another tack at the middle of the back rail. Tack down the remainder of the edges working from the centre outwards, and finally tack down the loose ends of the webs referred to above.

The stuffing can be hair or fibre, handfuls of which are pushed under bridle ties. These are shown in Fig 5 and are loops of twine

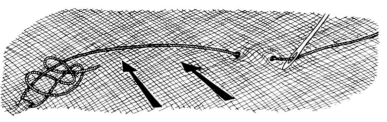

Bridle ties & running stitch

Fig 5 Sewing bridle ties.

just large enough for a hand to be pushed under. To make one, thread a mattress needle with twine and make a knot about 3in (76mm) away from both edges at one of the corners. Continue all round the seat at the same distance in from the edges, making a small stitch through the hessian between the loops. Concentrate on keeping most of the stuffing at the centre so that it does not hang over the edges and aim for a nicely rounded, slightly domed shape.

Next cover this with calico, allowing about 1in (25mm) all round for tacking off on the underside of the frame. Hold the calico in place temporarily with partly driven tacks, starting at the centre and working outwards smoothing the fabric as you go, and allowing about 3in (76mm) gaps between tacks. When you are satisfied that the calico is smooth and taut, tack it down finally on the underside, removing the temporary tacks as you come to them.

The last step is to fit and tack down the final cover in the same way, bearing in mind that if it is patterned, all the seats must match. A piece of black canvas tacked over the underside provides a neat finish.

Loose seat – modern method

Having made the seat frame as already described, there are several kinds of modern stuffing materials available. These include rubberized hair, fibre and cotton linters that are already fixed to hessian backings to form a suitable size of pad, so avoiding the need for bridle ties and hand stuffing (although you will still need the calico cover).

Fig 6(A) shows a loose seat frame fitted with serpentine (zigzag) springing; the detail at (B) shows how a length of spring is fitted into a clip which is nailed to the frame. It is a very efficient method and when covered with one of the stuffing pads described above it makes a comfortable seat; it can also be covered with a layer of 1in (25mm) resilient plastic foam.

Negotiating corners

Fig 7(A) shows the recommended way to finish the corners of a loose seat, while (B) and (C) illustrate how to deal with square and rounded corners respectively; (D) shows how the cover is fitted around a backfoot.

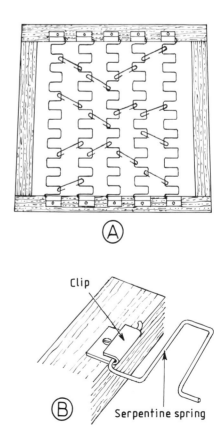

Clip

Serpentine spring

Fig 6 Serpentine springing.

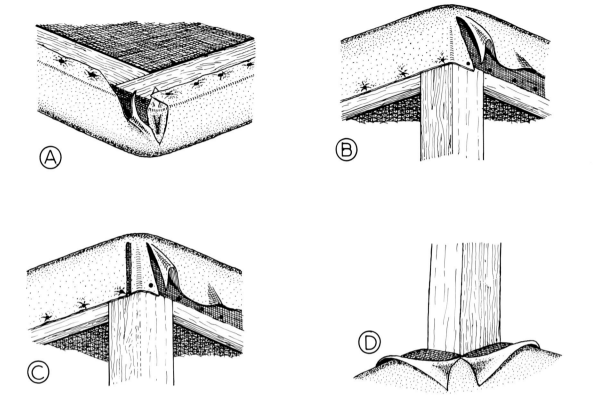

Fig 7 How to cut and fit the cover around (A) loose seat corners; (B) square corners; (C) rounded corners; (D) a backfoot.

Sprung seat

This would be suitable for the George III Elbow Chair on pages 11–15. The first step is to fix the webbing to the underside of the chair seat and then fix some 4in or 5in (102mm or 127mm) double cone springs to them. Fig 8(A) shows how to arrange the interlaced webs (called 'checking' in the trade) and tack them on to the frame, and also the sequence of fixing the springs with twine. You will need to tie a slip knot at the start, carrying on with three half-hitches round each spring, and finishing with a double-hitch; all three knots are illustrated in Fig 8(B).

The next stage is to lash the springs together at the top with laid cord or twine; laid cord is a special twine made so that it will not stretch and is preferable if available. Tap in two ⅝in (16mm) improved tacks, one at the centre of the top edge of the front rail and one in the centre of the back, both being only partly driven home. Lay a length of laid cord over the springs from back to front and after allowing an extra 12in (305mm) or so as a working allowance, cut it off. Using a slip-knot, make a loop at one end and put it over the tack in the back rail, pull it tight and hammer the tack down. Bring the cord forward, tying it to the springs with half-hitches until you reach the tack at the front where you make a double-hitch round it, hammering it down and cutting off any excess.

Repeat the procedure along each row of springs so that the final result looks like Fig 9; the important point is that the springs should not be compressed but fixed to prevent them moving sideways. Finish this stage by laying a piece of hessian over the springs, trimming it to size and then fastening the springs to it in the same way as you fastened them to the webbing.

To complete the job add the same stuffing as for the loose seat, using a similar method to fix it.

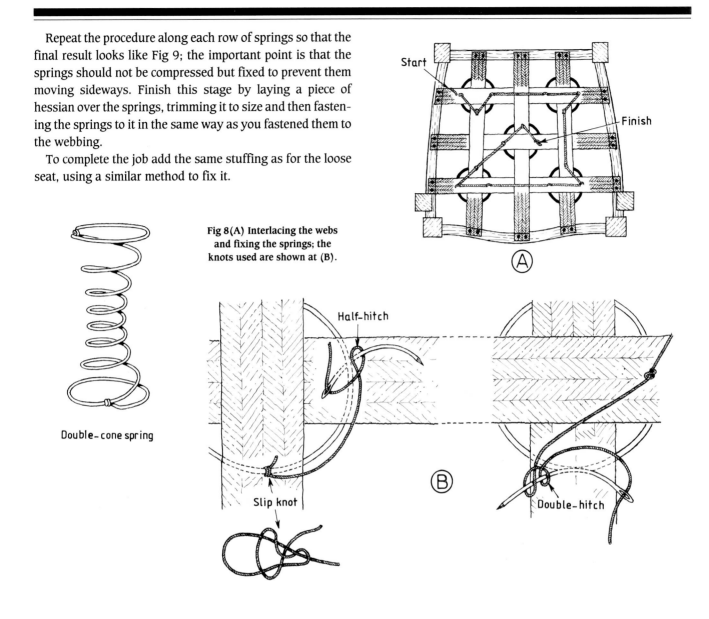

Start

Finish

Fig 8(A) Interlacing the webs and fixing the springs; the knots used are shown at (B).

Ⓐ

Double-cone spring

Half-hitch

Slip knot

Ⓑ

Double-hitch

Fig 9 How the springs should look when fixing is complete.

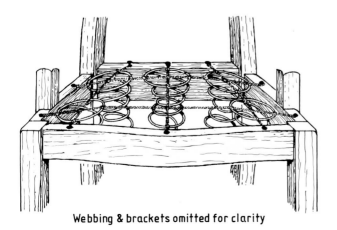

Webbing & brackets omitted for clarity

LIST OF SUPPLIERS – UK

Cabinet fittings and brassware

J. D. Beardmore & Co Ltd (head office), Field End Rd, Ruislip, Middx, HA4 0QG, Tel 081 864 6811. Shops at: 3–5 Percy St, London, W1P 0EJ, Tel 071 637 7041; 49 Park St, Bristol, Tel 0272 27831; and 120 Western Rd, Hove, Sussex, Tel 0273 71801. Period brassware for furniture, doors, and windows.

General Woodwork supplies, 76–80 Stoke Newington High St, London, N16 5BR, Tel 071 254 6052. General range of cabinet fittings.

Charles Greville & Co Ltd, Willey Mill House, Alton Rd, Farnham, Surrey, GU10 5EL, Tel 0252 715481. Brass finials, spandrels, and hinges.

Optimum Brasses, 7 Castle St, Bampton, Devon, Tel 0398 31515. Antique brass fittings; will make to order.

Romany Tyzack, 52–56 Camden High Street, London NW1 0LT, Tel 071 387 2579. Comprehensive range of period and modern brassware, including brass and wooden gallery rails. The firm is part of the Tyzack Retail Group which has branches as follows (full addresses in Yellow Pages): Parker Tyzack at Catford, London; Parry Tyzack at Old Street, London and Borough High Street, London; Hall Tyzack at Merton, London, and Bath, Bristol, Cardiff, Plymouth and Taunton.

H. E. Savill, 9 St Martin's Place, Scarborough, North Yorkshire, YO11 2QH, Tel 0723 373032. Probably the widest stocks of all the suppliers of period brassware.

Woodfit Ltd, Kem Mill, Chorley, Lancs, PR6 7EA, Tel 02572 66421. A really comprehensive range of cabinet and kitchen furniture fittings; some period brassware. Their catalogue is indispensable.

World of Wood, The Art Veneers Co Ltd, Industrial Estate, Mildenhall, Suffolk, IP28 7AY, Tel 0638 712550. Some period brassware and cabinet fittings. Their catalogue is well worth having.

Leather tops

S. Doctors, 5a Lansdown Mews, Farm Rd, Hove, Sussex, Tel 0273 774630.

Dorn Antiques, Tew Lane, Wootton, Woodstock, Oxon, OX7 1HA, Tel 0993 812023.

World of Wood (address above).

Finishes, oils, polishes, sealers, stains, varnishes, and waxes

Fiddes, Brindley Rd, Cardiff, CF1 7TX, Tel 0222 340323.

House of Harbru, 101 Crostons Rd, Elton, Bury, Lancs, BL8 1AL, Tel 061 764 6769.

Liberon Waxes Ltd, 6 Park St, Lydd, Kent, Tel 0679 20107/21299. Waxes plus general polishing supplies.

John Myland Ltd, 80 Norwood High St, London, SE27 9NW, Tel 081 670 9161. Can supply adhesives and abrasives as well as polishing materials.

Poth, Hille & Co Ltd, High St, Stratford, London, E15 2QD, Tel 081 534 2291. All kinds of waxes, especially rare ones.

Weaves and Waxes, 53c Church St, Bloxham, Banbury, Oxon, OX15 4ET, Tel 0295 721535. Good range of waxes.

World of Wood (address above). Usual polishing materials.

Special tools

Alec Tiranti Ltd, 70 High St, Theale, Reading, Berks, RG7 5AR, Tel 0734 302775. Also at 27 Warren St, London, W1P 5DG. Wood carving tools and equipment.

Ashley Iles (Edge Tools) Ltd, East Kirkby, Spilsby, Lincs, PE23 4DD, Tel 07903 372. Wood carving and turning tools.

Peter Child, The Old Hyde, Little Yeldham, Essex, CO9 4QT, Tel 0787 237291. Wood turning tools and pyrographic equipment.

Henry Taylor Tools Ltd, The Forge, Lowther Rd, Sheffield, S6 2DR, Tel 0742 340282/340321. Wood carving tools.

World of Wood (address above). Veneering and marquetry tools.

Exotic and decorative timbers and mouldings

Mackintosh Craftwoods, Unit 7, Fort Fareham, Newgate Lane, Fareham, Hants, Tel 0329 221925.

MHL Specialwoods Ltd, Beldray Park, Bilston, West Midlands, WV14 7NH, Tel 0902 353733.

Milland Fine Timber Ltd, Milland Pottery, Milland, Liphook, Hants, GU30 7JP, Tel 042 876 505.

North East Hardwoods Ltd, Whisby Way, Lincoln, LN6 3QT, Tel 0522 501485.

Palmyre Ltd, Glasson Estate, Maryport, Cumbria, CA15 8NX, Tel 0900 812796. Suppliers of bamboo.

South West Hardwoods Ltd, Blackweir Terrace, Cardiff, CF1 3EQ, Tel 0222 382053.

Timberline, Unit 7, Munday Works, 58–66 Morley Rd, Tonbridge, Kent, TN9 1RP, Tel 0732 355626.

Winther Browne, Nobel Rd, Eley Estate, Edmonton, London, N18 3DX, Tel 081 803 3434. Antique mouldings.

Upholstery materials and tools

Bostock Woodcraft Ltd, 5 Fairfax Mews, Fairfax Rd, London, N8 0NH, Tel 081 341 2511.

Cope and Timmins Ltd, Angel Road Works, Edmonton, N18 3AY, Tel 081 803 6481.

Dunlop Ltd, Dunlop House, 25 Ryder St, St James's, London, SW1Y 6PX, Tel 071 930 6700. This is the head office from which you can obtain details of their products etc, and also several useful booklets containing technical information.

Romany Tyzack (addresses above).
Russell & Chapple Ltd, 23 Monmouth St, London WC2H 9DE, Tel 071 836 7521.

Veneers, marquetry decorations and bandings

R. Aaronson (Veneers) Ltd, 45 Redchurch St, London, E2 7DJ, Tel 071 739 3107.

J. Crispin & Sons, 92–96 Curtain Rd, Shoreditch, London, EC2A 3AA, Tel 071 739 4857.
Fiddes (address above).
General Woodwork Supplies (address above).
Mackintosh Craftwoods (address above).
MHL Specialwoods Ltd (address above).
Weaves & Waxes (address above).
World of Wood (address above).

LIST OF SUPPLIERS – USA

Antique brassware

Ball and Ball, 436 West Lincoln Highway, Exton, PA 19341.
Charolette Ford Trunks, PO Box 536, Spearman, TX 79081.
Crown City Hardware Co, 1047 North Allen Avenue, Pasadena, CA 91104.
Garrett Wade, 161 Avenue of the Americas, New York, NY 10013.
Horton Brasses Mfg, PO Box 120, Nooks Hill Rd, Cromwell, CT 06416.
Imported European Hardware, 4295 South Arville, Las Vegas, NV 89103.
Paxton Hardware, PO Box 256-AW 10, Upper Falls, MD 21156.
Woodcraft, 210 Wood County Industrial Park, PO Box 1686, Parkersburg, WV 26102–1686.

Chair caning, leather and upholstery

Berman Leathercraft, 25 Melcher St, Boston, MA 02210.
Caning Shop, 926–A. W. Gilman, Berkeley, CA 94710.
Jack's Upholstery & Caning Supplies, Oswego, IL 60543.
Shaker Workshops, PO Box 1028, Concord, MA 01742 and The Connecticut Cane & Reed Co, PO Box 1276, Manchester, CT 06040. Both can supply coloured tape for Shaker chair seats.

Gilding supplies

Fine Gold Leaf People, Three Cross St, Suffern, NY 10901.
The Gold Leaf People, 23 Lawrence, Spring Valley, NY 10977.

INDEX